No. 301   FOREIGN POLICY ASSOCIATION   Winter

Religious Fundamentalisms and Global Conflict

by R. Scott Appleby

Cover Design: Bob Mansfield $5.95

The Author

R. Scott Appleby is associate professor of history at the University of Notre Dame and director of its Cushwa Center for the Study of American Catholicism. He continues to codirect The Fundamentalism Project, a six-year international public-policy study conducted by the American Academy of Arts and Sciences. A historian of religion who earned a Ph.D. from the University of Chicago in 1985, he is the author of numerous books and articles and lectures frequently on modern world religions.

The Foreign Policy Association

The Foreign Policy Association is a private, nonprofit, nonpartisan educational organization. Its purpose is to stimulate wider interest and more effective participation in, and greater understanding of, world affairs among American citizens. Among its activities is the continuous publication, dating from 1935, of the Headline Series. The author is responsible for factual accuracy and for the views expressed. FPA itself takes no position on issues of U.S. foreign policy.

Headline Series (ISSN 0017-8780) is published four times a year, Spring, Summer, Fall and Winter, by the Foreign Policy Association, Inc., 729 Seventh Ave., New York, N.Y. 10019. Chairman, Paul B. Ford; President, John Temple Swing; Editor in Chief, Nancy L. Hoepli; Senior Editors, Ann R. Monjo and K.M. Rohan. Subscription rates, $20.00 for 4 issues; $35.00 for 8 issues; $50.00 for 12 issues. Single copy price $5.95; double issue $11.25. Discount 25% on 10 to 99 copies; 30% on 100 to 499; 35% on 500 to 999; 40% on 1,000 or more. Payment must accompany all orders. Postage and handling: $2.50 for first copy; $.50 each additional copy. Application to mail at second-class postage rates is pending at New York, N.Y., and additional mailing offices. POSTMASTER: Send address changes to Headline Series, Foreign Policy Association, 729 Seventh Ave., New York, N.Y. 10019. Copyright 1994 by Foreign Policy Association, Inc. Design by K.M. Rohan. Printed at Science Press, Ephrata, Pennsylvania. Winter 1992. Published April 1994.

Library of Congress Catalog Card No. 94-70363
ISBN 0-87124-157-9

FOREWORD

The Fundamentalism Project

In dedicating a large portion of a public-policy grant from the MacArthur Foundation to a six-year interdisciplinary study of religious fundamentalisms on five continents, the American Academy of Arts and Sciences was responding to the increasing significance of these forms of politicized religion. In 1988, the AAAS, a learned society composed of more than 3,000 distinguished scholars, artists and business leaders in the United States (with over 500 foreign honorary members), commissioned a team that grew to over 200 scholars, many of whom were recruited where fundamentalist movements are active. These Fundamentalism Project scholars held a series of public conferences from 1988 to 1993 and prepared five encyclopedic volumes (four of which have already been published by the University of Chicago Press) describing and analyzing the rise, impact and organizational dynamics of over three dozen movements from seven major religious traditions.

In establishing The Fundamentalism Project, the AAAS

was not pursuing a specific political objective or supporting any particular program. Rather, its action was prompted by an awareness that the various movements have been poorly understood, despite the fact that they play a significant role in global political and economic developments.

The AAAS chose a scholar of religion, Martin E. Marty of the University of Chicago, to lead the interdisciplinary project. The choice underscored the sponsor's view that foreign policy analysts and educators commit a serious error when they assume fundamentalism is, to quote a former U.S. State Department official, "essentially a sociopolitical protest movement sugarcoated with religious pieties." Clearly it is mistaken to assume that secular rationality is the exclusive mode of thought and discourse in international and inter-regional relations; or, that well-educated people are not capable of retaining a religious sensibility; or, that religious consciousness is subordinate to the authority of reason or economic self-interest. Yet such mistaken assumptions led to some spectacular blunders the U.S. foreign policy establishment made in the 1970s and 1980s.

Rushdie Death Sentence

As some diplomats discovered belatedly, many influential world leaders believe in and live by religious doctrine taken in its most literal meaning. When Iran's Ayatollah Ruhollah Khomeini issued a *fatwa* (religious-legal verdict) in 1989 sentencing Salman Rushdie, the Indian-born British novelist, to death for blaspheming Islam, the Iranian leader promised paradise to the author's executioner. Many Western analysts focused, predictably, on the possible political, economic and diplomatic rationales for Khomeini's decision. Some reasoned that the ayatollah was reasserting his position as the leader of revolutionary Islam in the Middle East and South Asia by dramatically condemning the prominent author whose novel *The Satanic Verses* had disgraced the memory of the Prophet. Others surmised that Khomeini was sending a signal of support to the hard-liners in the Iranian regime.

The late Ayatollah Ruhollah Khomeini was a genuine religious leader. Above, worshippers outside his home in East Tehran in 1979.

Shrewd political calculation was arguably a motive for Khomeini's condemnation of Rushdie. Yet the experts ignored a simple fact, scandalous to Western sensibilities but absolutely essential to a correct analysis of the situation: Khomeini was a genuine religious leader. As scholars specializing in religion were quick to point out, he saw the world through the eyes of an Islamic jurisprudent who believed himself to be the Supreme Jurist, obligated to govern the Islamic Republic of Iran in the absence of the Hidden Imam. In the conclusion of *Fundamentalisms and the State,* the third volume in The Fundamentalism Project series, it is noted that "Khomeini acted on faith—a faith shared by millions of Muslims who perpetuated the calumny on Rushdie long after the ayatollah passed from the scene. This shared faith remains a legitimating principle for putatively Islamic regimes, as well as for the post-Khomeini Islamic Republic of Iran." Had U.S. policymakers and media persons grasped this essential principle of politics in an Islamic regime, they would have realized that the decree of condemnation, and Iran's unswerving opposition to certain kinds of expressions of "free speech," would survive Khomeini's passing.

In an attempt to provide insight and information about this often overlooked element in international affairs, contributors to The Fundamentalism Project have emphasized the irreducible role of religion and authentic religious belief in several of the current regional and international conflicts.

1

The Surprising Resurgence
of Religion

In the 1960s many educated observers of society in the United States and other parts of the world were convinced that scientific progress was dooming religious people and religious communities to irrelevance. If religion were to survive at all, the commentators stated, it must become an exclusively private affair, divorced from discussions of public morality and eliminated from debates about international relations, educational systems, medical practices, economic policies and other matters of public concern. The privatization of religion was well under way and proceeding at a rapid pace in the late twentieth century.

The earliest predictions of religion's demise as a public force had come from eighteenth-century European philosophes locked in mortal combat with the Roman Catholic Church. The French philosopher Voltaire, for example, had assumed that in the future all education would be based on human reason rather than divine revelation and that the "age of enlightenment" would displace the superstitious and authoritarian religious order. Two hundred years later, Harvard theologian Harvey Cox celebrated *The Secular City,* and many of his colleagues in the study of religion proclaimed that religious communities must become secularized, adjusting their practices and beliefs to this world rather than to a world beyond time and space. Sociologists, in particular, embraced secularization to explain what seemed to be the waning influence of religion. They proclaimed the inevitable triumph of reason over revelation, of material progress over otherworldly hopes.

Today, in the last decade of the twentieth century, radical religion's doubters are not quite as confident as they were in the 1960s. Cox, among many others, notes the endurance of *Religion in the Secular City.* A survey of contemporary religious traditions demonstrates amply the reason for the loss of confidence in secularization theory: everywhere, it seems, from the United States to Latin America, from the Middle East to South Asia, from Africa to the republics of the former Soviet Union, religion is reasserting itself as the custodian of cultural values and the interpreter of everyday events for hundreds of millions of people. Rather than restrict itself to the solemn assemblies of the church, mosque, synagogue or temple, religion has expanded its hold on public attention, proclaiming loudly its power to inspire individuals and peoples. Indeed, for the millions of Muslim women who have returned to the veil and traditional dress, for the Christian pro-life political activists in the United States, and for the young citizens of India who openly campaign for a Hindu nation, the distinction between public and private spheres of life, with religion relegated to the latter, seems to hold little meaning.

The most important and prominent manifestations of a global religious resurgence are the fundamentalist and fundamentalistlike movements, which seek political power to complement and enforce their religious and cultural programs. Leaders embracing fundamentalist versions of Islam have come to power in Iran and the Sudan, and pose a challenge in other countries of the Middle East and North Africa. They are building on the deeply rooted cultural influence fundamentalists have exercised for a generation or, as in the case of Egypt, for generations. In India, three fundamentalistlike nationalist movements grouped under the banner of Hinduism are making political gains in local and national elections, even as they strive to narrow the legal rights of hundreds of millions of Indian citizens who are not Hindus. In Sri Lanka, militant Sinhalese Buddhist nationalists, led by radical monks, violently oppose the Tamil minority (mostly Hindu) and its separatist campaign, as well as the intervention of neighboring India on its behalf.

Fundamentalism and the Mideast Peace Accord

In regions where fundamentalists are not currently poised to take power, they may nonetheless wield considerable influence in determining the outcome of political struggles. Many policy analysts believe, for example, that Israel and the Palestine Liberation Organization (PLO)* finally came to the peace table in 1993 because of their mutual fear of the growing popularity and power of religious fundamentalists. No one doubts that the violent reaction of extremists on both sides to the historic agreement of September 13, 1993, which called for Israel's withdrawal from Jericho and the Gaza Strip, forced the extension of the deadline and threatened the overall implementation of the peace accord. One particularly vexing question for Israel was whether the PLO could fulfill its commitment to end the six-year-old *intifada* (Palestinian uprising) and control such extremist Islamic fundamentalist groups as Hamas* (Islamic Resistance Movement), Islamic Jihad and radical elements of the PLO's own Fatah organization, a secular entity. Israel, meanwhile, faces its own right-wing obstructionists, among them Jewish settlers in the occupied territories, some of whose leaders qualify as a Jewish face of fundamentalism. These religious-nationalist Jews refuse to yield one square foot of the "sacred land" promised to Israel by Yahweh in the Torah. The

*See glossary, p. 79.

9

heavily armed settlers have recently engaged in vigilantism—
the use of unauthorized violence—in retaliation for Palestinian attacks in the wake of the peace accord. On February 25,
1994, this practice culminated in the massacre of 29 Palestinian Muslims who were worshipping in the Cave of the Patri-
archs mosque in Hebron (in the occupied territories). The
lone assailant, Baruch Goldstein, was affiliated with Kach,
the party of the late Rabbi Meir Kahane, who advocated the
forceful expulsion of Arabs from the occupied territories.
Goldstein's single act of terror was designed to discredit
PLO leader Yasir Arafat and to derail the peace process
entirely.

While Islamic fundamentalists capture most of the headlines and hold the attention of many foreign-policy makers,
Hindu nationalists, Buddhist militants and Christian combat-
ants (such as the Protestant unionists and Catholic insurrec-
tionists in Northern Ireland) pose their own unique challenges to peace and stability in their homelands. It is little
wonder, then, that a State Department official predicted in
1991 that religious fundamentalism would be the major foreign policy concern for the United States in the 1990s.

Defining Fundamentalism

In order to come to a working definition of "fundamentalism" and to understand its role in global politics in the late
twentieth century, it is necessary to begin with an examination of the religious character of the phenomenon. What
kind of religion do fundamentalists espouse?

Fundamentalism is neither a "new religious movement"
(in the technical sense of the term) nor a "traditional," "conservative" or "orthodox" expression of religious faith and
practice. Rather, fundamentalism belongs in a category by itself. While fundamentalists claim to be upholding orthodoxy
(established belief) or orthopraxy (correctness of practice),
and to be defending age-old religious traditions and ways of
life from erosion, they do so by crafting new methods, formulating new ideologies and adopting the latest organiza-

**The White House, September 13, 1993: Israeli Prime Minister
Yitzhak Rabin and PLO chairman Yasir Arafat shake hands as President
Bill Clinton looks on. Mutual fear of the growing power of religious
fundamentalists played a role in bringing the two together.**

tional structures and processes. Some of these seem to violate the historic beliefs, interpretive practices and moral behavior of earlier generations—or, at the least, to depart significantly from these precedents. Indeed, fundamentalists often find fault with fellow believers who want to conserve tradition but are not willing to create new ways to fight the forces of erosion. In other words, fundamentalists argue that to be merely a conservative or a traditionalist in these threatening times is not enough.

At the same time, fundamentalists reject the suggestion that they are doing something radically new. A crucial element of their rhetoric and self-understanding is the assertion that their programs are based on the authority of the sacred past, represented in a privileged text or tradition or in the teaching of a charismatic or official leader. Fundamentalists do not have a special or distinctive longing for a simpler, less complex world. Yet they are careful to demonstrate the continuity between their programs and teachings and their religious heritage. A pronounced rootedness in scripture and/or "purified" tradition, coupled with a reluctance to embrace the New Age spiritualist movements, characterizes religious fundamentalism. Thus, for example, Christian fundamentalists, strictly speaking, do not belong to Pentecostal churches or movements, which rely heavily on prophecy, speaking in tongues and the leading of the Holy Spirit; similarly, one would not expect the Sufi* movements within Islam to produce Muslim fundamentalists, given the Sufi emphasis on mystical experience.

The twentieth century is characterized by a blending of distinct cultural and religious elements that affects even ultraconservative movements. In this cultural environment, borrowing and absorbing influences from disparate sources are common occurrences. Christian Pentecostals and bible-believing fundamentalists make common cause for political purposes; Sufi mystics swell the ranks of Muslim fundamentalist movements; Hindu nationalists borrow religious structures and concepts from Judaism, Christianity and Islam. Such borrowing, mixing and matching are tactical necessities in the battle fundamentalists are waging against secular modernity. They are seeking to hold ground against spreading secular contamination and even to regain ground by taking advantage of the weaknesses of modernization.

The blanket use of the term "fundamentalism" to encompass these global phenomena creates problems, since all religious movements are shaped by the ideological and organizational properties of their host traditions, and they are constrained by cultural, economic and political conditions. Not all religious traditions make clear separations between the sacred and the secular, have the same kinds of institutions, assume "end-times" deliverance by a savior or a messiah, or have clearly formulated doctrines and codes imputed to divine origin. Nor have all religious traditions been confronted in the same way and degree by modernity and secularism. As political scientist Gabriel A. Almond has explained: "Secular modernity may have been introduced endogenously [from within the society] in Europe and North America, through the industrial, technological and scientific revolutions, or it may have been introduced by ethnoreligiously alien, imperialistic and exploitative forces as in the Middle East, Asia, Africa and Latin America. The program and organization of fundamentalist movements will have been affected by the auspices and structure of the secular threat to their survival, on the one hand, and the structure and composition of their religious tradition, on the other."

Roots of Revivalism: Religion and Culture

Thus, the fundamentalisms of Protestant and Roman Catholic Christianity, Sunni* and Shiite* Islam, and Judaism will differ in important respects in view of their different histories, and they will be alike in certain other respects by virtue of their sharing the traditions going back to Abraham—monotheism, messianism, and sacred, codified doctrine and law. It is easier to establish a fundamentalist movement when religious tenets are spelled out explicitly in sacred texts and codes. What is called fundamentalism in South Asia will bear the marks of the Hindu, Sikh* and Buddhist religions, as well as the history of the various parts of the area. It should not surprise us that the concept "fundamentalism" is "culture bound" and that family resemblances become strained the farther the distance between a fundamentalist movement and the point at which it was named and acquired its identity. "Religion is not the only matrix out of which fundamentalistlike movements emerge. Race, language and culture may also serve as the bases of revivalism and militance," Almond writes. "It is not unusual for ethnicity and religion to combine, as in Hinduism. Hindu fundamentalism is ethno-nationalist as well as religious. The two spheres are not neatly separated."

Given the diversity of expressions of fundamentalism and

their overlap with ethnic and nationalist forces in some cases, it is not surprising that foreign policy experts have only recently begun to comprehend this complex phenomenon. Such an understanding, however, is important in the tumultuous post-cold-war world. The collapse of the Soviet Union and the superpower rivalry has ended not only the cold war but also the structures that provided a measure of stability and predictability in geopolitics in the decades after World War II. Fundamentalism introduces an unpredictable element to the "new world order" because its appeal, at least in part, is based on religious worldviews rather than the more familiar political ideologies.

'Riddle Wrapped in a Mystery'

Because fundamentalism is diverse in expression and form, rather than one monolithic reality, some scholars and religious leaders are understandably uneasy accepting any generalizations, however nuanced, about the phenomenon. Rather than borrow an American term to describe religious movements and individuals of other cultures—Middle Eastern, African, Asian and South Asian—they deny fundamentalism's existence apart from the Protestant Christian movement in the United States, where the word originated. Others acknowledge the presence of fundamentalism, but disagree about its characteristics. Despite dissenting voices, the term "fundamentalism," as used by many Western journalists, scholars and religious leaders, refers to a distinct expression of modern religiopolitics, or political religion. Interestingly, many Middle Easterners and Asians have adopted the word. Moreover, the importance of global fundamentalisms and their political and social impact has also given rise to a growing number of scholarly and public-policy studies that compare similar movements in various religious traditions.

In these studies one finds various, and overlapping, definitions of fundamentalism. Yet, "fundamentalist" usually conveys "religious" rather than "secular," "intolerant" rather than "ecumenical," "militant" rather than "moderate." Obviously, however, one must qualify the term, lest law-abiding Christians or Muslims or Jews be lumped together with regimes or movements that systematically oppress, torture or even execute their opponents. "Fundamentalist" connotes a certain kind of believer who wishes to form or defend a state or society based in some explicit way upon sacred history, laws, customs, traditions and/or moral obligations. Yet there are both moderate fundamentalists, who work within the law to achieve these ends, and radical fundamentalists, who adopt extralegal means and resort to violence.

In the case of Egypt, for example, the Muslim Brotherhood, founded in 1928, presently represents the moderate mainstream of the Islamic current: it recently organized a demonstration protesting the actions of extremist (or "radical fundamentalist") groups against Christian citizens in Egypt. With qualifications, fundamentalism describes the central process involved in constructing a late-twentieth century militant politicized religion. The leaders are often graduates of secular academies or universities; they tend to specialize in engineering or medicine, and are quite at home with modern technologies, political processes and the latest strategies of mass-marketing and mobilization. Although relatively well-educated, many young men who are attracted to the fundamentalist movements feel they have been cheated by society and its leaders. The privileged elites—educators, scientists, politicians—have manifestly failed either to share the wealth or preserve traditional markers of home, family and communal identity, be these prayer in the school, an exclusively domestic role for women, or literal belief in things unseen. Thus the fundamentalists reach back to retrieve elements of a sacred tradition that they claim to be absolutely fundamental or essential to the faith. These new fundamentals, taken out of their historical context, then become melded with modern bureaucratic, political or military concepts. The religious fundamentals are interpreted or "constructed" in the way most useful to the ideological and organizational goals of the movement.

Fundamentalisms' Religious Characteristics

Although fundamentalists are in the minority in each religious tradition, they compete effectively with nonfundamentalists for the attention of the popular media. Employing the tactics of minority and protest groups seeking representation in the court of public opinion, fundamentalists have a flair for dramatic, symbolic action that lends itself readily to countercultural activism, political engagement, and, at times, violence. Although fundamentalists are not always so engaged, their distinctive form of religious conviction reflects a tendency to want to remake "the world"—narrowly defined as their religious enclave or broadly conceived as the larger, pluralistic society. Such an endeavor requires charismatic and authoritarian leadership and a disciplined inner core of adherents who follow a rigorous moral code. Fundamentalists set sharp boundaries, identify and aggrandize the enemy, seek converts, and build institutions dedicated to advancing the program of reconstituting society at large.

Religious idealism plays a key role in religious fundamentalist movements. This is not true of other social protest movements of this century, such as the PLO or the Shining Path guerrillas of Peru, or other movements influenced by Marxism. Marxist movements in particular are not concerned with a transcendent realm and a divine law. In Islam and Judaism, by contrast, the revealed law provides an irreducible basis for communal and personal identity. In Protestant Christianity, the "born-again" experience serves a similar function: through the conversion experience one enters into a new life and identity that is "guaranteed" by an authority greater than any human precept or individual.

This "celestial aspiration" orients the true believer to a pragmatic program of action. Muslim fundamentalists thus strive to implement God's will as expressed in the religious-moral law, the Sharia,* culled from the Quran* (also written as Koran) and the Hadith, or traditions, of the Prophet

16

Muhammad. Jewish radicals interpret political events according to the prophecies of the Hebrew scriptures. And, despite a radically different view of the relationship between the eternal and the temporal, Theravada Buddhist fundamentalists in Sri Lanka also believe that their identity is "rooted in the very nature of being and the cosmos and thus beyond the reach of human temporal and spatial considerations and the relativizing force of history," according to historian of religion Donald K. Swearer of Swarthmore College.

For many if not all religious people, not just fundamentalists, the integrity of religious identity depends on the reliability of divine revelation. The source of that revelation may be the Quran, the Bible, or the Sikh holy book, the Granth Sahib.* For the fundamentalist, the sacred text is a blueprint for sociopolitical action as well as a guide to spiritual life. In looking to the sacred text for direction in public action, fundamentalists prefer to accept the literal meaning. Or, if the text requires interpretation (as it usually does), it is to be made by a cleric, scholar or rabbi—a duly constituted religious authority—who will not water down or explain away the radical, prophetic, supernatural character of the text. In fact, the supernatural character of revelation is particularly important to the fundamentalist sense of identity in that it connotes a way of knowing and a source of truth that are essentially superior to those of the secular scientist or philosopher. Belief in things unseen is considered unreliable in secular pursuits; fundamentalists make it the central tenet of their identity.

Fundamentalists are not necessarily different from other believers in the content of the doctrines they hold; for example, most nonfundamentalist Christians believe in the bodily resurrection of Christ. But fundamentalists are more concerned than others with making explicit affirmation of such doctrines a requirement for inclusion in the company of true believers; the presumption is that fundamentalists alone enjoy privileged access to absolute truth. And because revealed truth is whole, unified and undifferentiated, one

17

may not pick and choose from among doctrines and practices. Thus fundamentalists resist compromise on these central doctrines and/or practices.

Fundamentalist leaders do their defining by pointing out the errant ways of those outside the pale; they are boundary-setters, concerned with the preservation of purity and preoccupied with separating the true believer from the pretender, the children of light from the children of darkness. Dualism plays an important role in the ideology of such movements, and boundary-setting takes many forms. One is the delineation and renaming of a plot of land or a contested site, claiming it as sacred space exclusively reserved (by God) for the true believers. For radical Sikhs in northern India, the Punjab is Khalistan (Land of the Pure); for the religious Zionists of the Jewish settler movement Gush Emunim (Bloc of the Faithful),* the West Bank is part of the biblical Judea and Samaria. Another way to signal "chosenness" is to adopt distinctive, symbolic dress. For Sikhs fighting against Hindus and Muslims in the Punjab, unshorn hair and short pants separate the pure from the impure; for the Gush Emunim, prayer shawls and long beards, combined with jeans or military fatigues, accomplish the same result.

The religious idealism and absolutism of fundamentalism also go a long way toward explaining its unique patterns of activism. Fundamentalists often see themselves as actors in an end-times drama unfolding in the mind of God and directing the course of human history. Iranian Shiites endure the injustice of the temporal order as they await the appearance of the just ruler, the Hidden Imam, at the end of time; or, in his absence, they follow a divinely designated successor (Ayatollah Khomeini) into militant activism. Ultra-Orthodox Jews in Israel's Mea Shearim neighborhood are long-suffering devotees of a messiah; until the day when the messiah comes, they consider themselves "in exile" in this world and shun human efforts to hasten the final redemption. In this they differ from the Jewish settlers in the occupied territories, who believe that God is directing them to take action now on His behalf (and who consider themselves no less orthodox for so believing). Christian fundamentalists in the twentieth century have also disagreed among themselves on specific interpretations of God's will for the final days, but they are in general agreement that these are the end-times, and that true believers must prepare in a very special way for the coming apocalypse.

Asia's Sacred Texts and Religious Icons

Sacred texts and apocalyptic scenarios do not play the same role in South Asian and Far Eastern traditions as they do in the Abrahamic faiths. In the Eastern traditions, history is not seen as a structured drama proceeding inexorably to a climactic final act. Thus it is noteworthy that several South Asian and Far Eastern fundamentalistlike movements depart from the practice of their host religious traditions and do in fact revere a sacred text and draw certain "fundamentals"—behaviors as well as beliefs—from it. For example, charismatic leaders of Japan's New Religions are sometimes called messiahs and deal in prophecy and soothsaying. In India, Hindu nationalists have chosen one mythical figure, Rama, from among India's vast array of deities and cast him as a modern-day nationalist icon, replete with all the trappings of an Old Testament prophet warning people of imminent destruction (in this case, destruction to be visited upon India if it does not mend its religiously plural and secular ways). The Hindu fundamentalists thereby create religious boundaries and fundamentals where none existed.

Missionary zeal is also characteristic of many fundamentalist groups. Believers who relax the guard, form coalitions with nonfundamentalists or de-emphasize the importance of conversion are often the first people to arouse fundamentalist ire. When Protestant Christian fundamentalists left other denominations at the beginning of the twentieth century, notes sociologist Nancy T. Ammerman, they frequently took their missionary zeal with them and invested it in agencies throughout the world. Whereas denominations were struggling, fundamentalist mission efforts around the world grew by leaps and bounds.

"Conversion" means different things in different cultures. In India or the Middle East, for example, an entire tribe or village might be won over to a new way of life; elsewhere the individual is the object of fundamentalist missionary efforts. Further, conversion to a distinct and all-encompassing way of life under the supervision of a religious and moral authority figure may or may not have immediate political implications. Demands on new "recruits" may be limited to their personal piety and religious observances, or they may be expected to express their religious zeal by political activism. In both cases, however, fundamentalists seem to thrive on confrontation with nonbelievers. While it is true that many types of social movements depend on an adversary to build group solidarity, fundamentalists specialize in studying their enemies. Whether they see their task as making converts and winning souls (to use the Christian term), or defending their way of life and view of morality, fundamentalists name, dramatize and mythologize the enemy, placing oppressive dictators or Westernized elites or compromising coreligionists within the same realm or "morality play" scenario in which they see themselves. To the followers of Khomeini and his Iranian successors, for example, the United States is not merely a superpower, but "the Great Satan."

Why does this dramatization occur? If conflicts between nation-states are understood in strictly secular political terms and thereby reduced to episodes in an unending series of international political conflicts—conflicts, say, over the control of oil prices, or geographical borders, or the definition of ethnic rights and privileges within a region—then politics remains a game of elites, of experts who have little personal, and certainly no spiritual, stake in outcomes. Compromise of principle is a standard feature of such politics. As a religious fundamentalist leader might say, in such politics one's soul is at risk. The soul and integrity of a people may be at risk when a cultural and spiritual heritage is compromised

Sheik Omar Abdel Rahman, the religious scholar who was indicted in connection with the World Trade Center bombing in February 1993, at his home in Jersey City, N.J., days before the attack.

Reuters/Bettmann

merely for material ends. When, for example, the state-supported university hires a faculty member for his or her technical expertise, or connection to a corporate donor, without regard for the person's religious orthodoxy, something dear to the religious sensibility is lost. When television or radio carries advertisements for liquor and risqué videos in sequence with a spot presenting the Muslim call to prayer, the integrity of religious identity is seen to be under insidious assault, prompting protests by fundamentalist ideologues. Because secular political leaders in much of the developing world have given short shrift to the need to conserve the cultural and spiritual heritage of a people and to protect the institutions embodying it, crises of a material as well as a spiritual nature have arisen. The problem at root is spiritual; the enemy, in its true face, is spiritual—unnaturally strong, possessed of supernatural powers that can be countered only by the virtuous believers relying on equally powerful spiritual antidotes.

Fundamentalist rhetoric elevates world events to this spiritual plane. Thus Christian fundamentalists, such as best-selling author Anton Walvoord of Dallas Theological Seminary in Texas, characterized the Persian Gulf war as a possible prelude to Armageddon, the Final Battle prophesied in Revelation, the last book of the New Testament. While his beliefs and practices are worlds apart from those of fundamentalist Christians in Dallas, Sheik Omar Abdel Rahman, the blind religious scholar charged with inspiring the conspiracy to blow up the World Trade Center in New York City in 1993, also invests historic events with a specific spiritual apocalyptic significance. Sheik Rahman believes that Egypt has descended into a state of *jahiliyyah,* a period of ignorance, and that as a result all pious Muslims are obliged to name and attack the new infidel who parades as a Muslim but who is in fact the enemy of true Islam. For Sheik Rahman, the enemy to be named and attacked is the president of the pseudo-Islamic state of Egypt, Hosni Mubarak, and, by extension, any government that supports his corrupt un-Islamic regime.

Placing the analysis of the religious content of fundamentalisms at the center of a working definition is the key to understanding fundamentalism as a social and political as well as religious phenomenon. However, the social, political, economic and cultural contexts in which this type of religious protest movements arise cannot be ignored. Indeed these contexts have a relevance of their own, quite apart from the "spin" given them by fundamentalist ideologues.

2

The Rise and Social
Dynamics of Fundamentalism

In certain respects, fundamentalist movements are like any social movements seeking political power. Thus they attract their fair share of people who are vengeful and exploitative, the "Oppressed of the Earth" (as one radical Shiite group called itself), eager for payback time to commence. Fundamentalisms also tend to attract people who are motivated more by a quest for power, prestige or wealth than by a commitment to the values espoused by the movement. In such cases religion is seldom more than the latest and perhaps most convenient vehicle for self-aggrandizement or for class revolt.

Usually, however, motivations are less pure and more complex. While all opposition or protest movements tend to swell in numbers under conditions of severe economic crisis and social displacement, fundamentalist movements appear to be particularly successful in exploiting widespread social discontent. Why is it that increasing numbers of people in South Asia, the Middle East and Africa opt for religious radicalism rather than some other form of social protest, especially when the religious movements are often politically inexperienced and untested? One answer seems to be that many people, especially in developing countries with a history of corruption on the part of government officials, feel that economic or social programs without moral or religious considerations sooner or later prove to be bankrupt morally and materially. While social and economic grievances are among the motivations for joining a fundamentalist movement, fundamentalisms also attract idealistic and well-educated young adults who are genuinely (and even primarily) concerned about the moral failures of their societies and who believe that the answer lies in a return to religious values and life-styles. Older adherents may be veterans of secular protest movements, as is the case with the ex-Marxist Adil Hussein, a prominent leader of Egypt's Muslim Brotherhood.

The growth of Islamic fundamentalism in Egypt was spurred by social and economic developments in the 1970s and 1980s similar to those occurring in much of the Sunni Arab world. Both the Muslim Brotherhood and its radical splinter groups attracted graduates of the state-run educational system. The secularized schools in Egypt were far more developed than the economy, which could not assimilate the waves of qualified technicians, managers and engineers they turned out during these decades. Many thousands of young men found themselves unemployed or stuck in bureaucratic backwaters, impoverished and unable to marry or raise a family. The government seemed unwilling or unable to provide meaningful options. For many graduates, Islam became the solution.

Another answer to the question of "Why fundamentalisms now?" turns on the sociological concept of "relative deprivation." This insight holds that people feel deprived not only when they have little or nothing at all, but also when they have sufficient means but see the status of other classes or social groups in their society improving, perhaps rapidly, while theirs has remained steady or perhaps even fallen a bit. (In either case, their status has fallen relative to other groups and so they feel relatively deprived.) In this context, leaders of the relatively deprived may turn to fundamentalisms. Historically, religion has protected the status quo and given comfort and justification to the privileged at least as frequently as it has inspired revolution and social-class upheaval. Fundamentalist religion may therefore function to check the upward mobility of despised classes or castes.

Hindu Fundamentalism and Class Warfare

Indeed, this seems to be the case in the late twentieth-century rise of Hindu fundamentalism, also known as Hindu nationalism, in India. In an insightful essay published in the March 22, 1993, issue of *The New Republic,* Susanne Hoeber Rudolph and Lloyd I. Rudolph, political scientists at the University of Chicago, argue that the hatred fueling the recent violent confrontations between Hindus and Muslims has less to do with ancient religious animosities than with modern class warfare. Indeed, the animosities were largely invented, the Rudolphs argue, by political manipulators who sought to take advantage of the resentment on the part of the old, established Hindu middle class of a rapidly rising new middle class composed of lower castes and Muslims—that is, groups previously outside the economic mainstream. Hindu nationalist politicians of the Bharatiya Janata party (BJP)* exploited the rift by "theologizing" it. The cultural wing of the BJP staged protests and riots in Ayodhya, a small town in eastern Uttar Pradesh (India's most populous state) at the site of a mosque built in the sixteenth century by the first Mughal emperor, Babur. According to the Hindu activists, Babur's Mosque stood on the birthplace of Lord Rama, and they urged that the mosque be destroyed and a temple (re)built on the site. The agitation led to the destruction of the mosque in December 1992, a cataclysmic event that sparked retaliatory violence resulting in the death of more than 2,500 people, most of them Muslims.

"One of the ways to think about the recent savaging of the Babri Masjid (Babur's Mosque) by young Hindu men," wrote the Rudolphs, "is to see it as a renegotiation of political and economic power and status, or rather as a sign of the pathology of renegotiation." Indians in the 1980s and early 1990s experienced unprecedented social mobility and economic growth as a consequence of the development and export of high-yield varieties of wheat (the Green Revolution), the growth of public-sector jobs, and other policies of liberalization. The lower castes and Muslims who profited from these advancements demanded quotas in government jobs and in schools. When these demands found a response in the implementation of Prime Minister V. P. Singh's 1990 Mandal Commission report, upper-caste students, fearful of losing job opportunities, raged against the mandated job quotas for minorities by burning buses, obstructing traffic, staging immolation rituals and forcing shops to close. The BJP stoked the fire by organizing a 6,000-mile pilgrimage to Ayodhya to build the Ram temple. Reflecting on the eventual destruction of the mosque, the Rudolphs commented:

> The youths we saw standing on the domes of the doomed mosque were wearing city clothes, shirts and trousers, not the *kurta* and *dhotis* of villagers or the urban poor....They are the educated unemployed, not the poor and illiterate. Frustrated by the lack of good jobs and opportunities, they are victims of modernization, seeking to victimize others—like "pampered" Muslims. In an India where, despite its problems, the number of persons under the poverty line has been declining and entrepreneurship expanding exponentially, their expectations have run well ahead of available opportunities.

In such an environment, where the rapid upward mobility of lower classes and castes breeds upper-caste envy and resentment, discrimination is justified in religious-communal rather than class-caste terms. In north India, Kerala and Bombay, where Muslim prosperity has also bred feelings of relative

Hindu protesters attack Babur's Mosque in Ayodhya, India, on October 30, 1990. These fundamentalists want to replace the mosque with a temple to Lord Rama.

deprivation, Hindus decry "Nehru-style secularism" as "privileging Muslim communalism and stigmatizing Hindu communalism." This is our country after all, is the indignant cry of the discomfited Hindu elite. Muslims in turn have responded by bolstering their own militant fundamentalist organizations.

As this example suggests, besieged groups on several points of the political compass may find great use for religious identity retrieved and constructed on the "fundamentalist style."

Their religious character makes fundamentalists particularly skilled in analyzing and responding to profound human need. As shown in the examples from India and Egypt, fundamentalisms arise or come to prominence in times of crisis, actual or perceived. The sense of danger may be keyed to threatening social, economic or political conditions, but the ensuing crisis is perceived as a crisis of identity. The late nineteenth and twentieth centuries have brought rapid urbanization, modernization and uneven rates of development in much of the developing world. The vulnerability of masses of people to totalitarian dictators and military regimes in this era, the social and economic dislocation and deprivation attendant upon migration to the cities, the conditions of misery and exploitation experienced by millions of subject peoples—all these conditions have provided an opening for alternative philosophies and institutions.

Latin American Pentecostals

One striking example is found in the recent growth of Pentecostal communities in Latin America, many of which embrace the biblical literalism, moral absolutism, separatism and premillennialism previously associated with the independent churches established earlier in the century by North American fundamentalist missionaries. Traditional Roman Catholicism, with its foreign (i.e., European) clergy, reserved style of worship, and a strong identification with the landed classes and the corrupt and oppressive power elite, bore the brunt of fundamentalist anger and was the clear loser in this conversion of peoples to evangelicalism. While the new Latin American Pentecostal communities vary widely, they share with fundamentalisms elsewhere an emphasis on indigenous leadership and local responses to local problems in a time of crying human need. In *Fundamentalisms Observed,* Pablo Deiros, Argentinian historian of Christianity, describes the plight of the rural migrants in Latin American cities after World War II :

> Uprooted from families and religious traditions, living in slums and at the mercy of criminals and sometimes governmental predators, the urban poor became a fertile seedbed for evangelical proselytism. The weakening of traditional social controls, the sense of confusion and helplessness in the anonymity of city life, the shock of new social values sometimes accompanying the adaptation to industrial work, the absence of familiar community loyalties and of the encompassing paternalism still characteristic of rural employment—all these

conditions favored the growth of an acute crisis of personal identity for the migrants. Under such conditions, the exchange of old religious values for new ones was (and remains) likely to occur.

The fact that the new evangelicals and fundamentalists in Latin America come from the impoverished marginal classes and tend to be apolitical, quite unlike their North American counterparts, only underscores fundamentalism's serviceability for a variety of economic classes and political orientations.

In the rhetoric of crisis is often embedded a justification for extreme measures: fundamentalists seek to replace existing structures with a comprehensive system emanating from religious principles and embracing law, polity, society, economy and culture. This is particularly true where fundamentalism has arisen in the scores of nations that have emerged in the decades following World War II. (The fundamentalist drive to comprehensive structural change is, accordingly, less prevalent in a society like that of the United States, where existing institutions and civil society are strong and less readily bent to radical ends.) In Pakistan, independent since 1947, the fundamentalist party Jamaat-e-Islami, which calls for an Islamic state based on a national consensus, and other fundamentalist movements characterize Islam as a comprehensive way of life that covers the entire spectrum of human activity, be it individual, social, economic or political. By contrast, the conservative ulema (i.e., the "professional" religious scholars, or "clergy") confine Islam to the observance of its five pillars (profession of faith, prayer, fasting, alms-giving and pilgrimage to Mecca). While many Muslims seek to participate in the political process as Muslims, notes political scientist Mumtaz Ahmad, "the fundamentalists aspire to *capture* political power and establish an Islamic state on the prophetic model. They are not content to act as pressure groups....They want political power because they believe that Islam cannot be implemented without the power of the state."

As lay scholars of Islam, leaders of such fundamentalist

movements are not theologians, but social thinkers and political activists. Of the more than 120 publications, for example, by the Jamaat-e-Islami's founder, Abu al-Ala Mawdudi, only one is on a purely theological issue. His entire commentary on the Quran reads like an Islamic legal-political text, providing guidance in the fields of constitutional, social, civil, criminal, commercial and international law. By providing Islamic discourse with a political vocabulary, Mawdudi's influence on contemporary Islamic fundamentalist groups has been pervasive. By defining "the Islamic system of life," "Islamic ideology," "the Islamic constitution," "the economic system of Islam" and "the political system of Islam," Mawdudi has subordinated all of the institutions of civil society and the state to the authority of divine law.

Protestant Fundamentalists vs. Secular Humanists

The crises in which fundamentalisms have flourished vary. North American Protestant fundamentalism, for example, emerged in sectors of the nation undergoing rapid urbanization and industrialization—the Northeast at the beginning of the twentieth century; the South and Southeast during the second half. However, fundamentalists north and south mobilized in the 1970s because they were concerned that secular elites had assumed control of national institutions and symbols. These secular humanists—so-called because they embraced what fundamentalists saw as a pseudoreligion, a philosophy of human progress that explicitly marginalized religious values—were threatening to unravel "the moral fabric" of the country. This threat became palpable to fundamentalists in the decade of crisis from 1963 (the year of the Supreme Court ban on prayer in public schools) to 1973 (the year the Supreme Court overturned restrictive abortion laws in 46 states). To fundamentalists, secular humanism seemed to infiltrate the public-school curriculum. The "new morality" led to sexual promiscuity and a culture of pornography and drugs. The nation endured a failure of self-confidence in the controversy over the Vietnam war (1963–75). The corruption of political institutions was epitomized by the 1974 Watergate scandal, which began when Republicans broke into Democratic party headquarters. While many Christian and Jewish believers were troubled by the moral failures of the nation and the seeming spread of "value-free" education, the fundamentalists considered the situation a crisis calling for a moment of decision. They spoke of a "battle of the mind," as political activist Timothy LaHaye put it, between secular humanism and the Judeo-Christian tradition, for the meaning of the nation itself.

Elsewhere in the world, personal and cultural crises occurred in a quest for a formula for national identity that would allow rival ethnic and religious blocs to exist peacefully within the same borders and under the same constitution. Fundamentalist leaders, among others, called attention to the repeated failures of national elites to ensure a secure identity for these competing factions. For example, when postcolonial liberal nationalism, and later, Arab socialism failed to lift the Egyptian masses out of poverty or defeat the Israeli army, Islamic fundamentalists (who had been providing alternative institutions and messages since the 1930s) explained the failure by pointing to (neglected) Islam as the one Arab ideology not derived from Western models. The fundamentalist implementation of the Sharia was the only authentic basis for a true Islamic state.

Internal Dynamics of Fundamentalist Movements

Fundamentalism has proven itself selectively traditional and modern. Fundamentalists select carefully from among the plethora of doctrines, practices and interpretations available in the tradition. The past is defined with a keen eye on the particular challenges of the present and the opportunities of the future. Fundamentalists subtly lift the old doctrines from their original context, embellish and institutionalize them, and employ them as ideological weapons against a hostile world. The Christian fundamentalist doctrine of biblical infallibility, for example, is the nineteenth-century

JIM MORIN
The Miami Herald

creation of Princeton theologians rather than the explicit doctrine of the sixteenth-century Protestant Reformation. The Princetonians developed the doctrine to preserve the traditional Christian belief in the divine origins of the Bible and to counter the advent of the Higher Criticism, a scholarly method of subjecting the Bible to literary, archaeological and other historical criteria in order better to understand its human origins.

In the process of interpreting the tradition, evaluating modernity and selectively retrieving salient elements of both, charismatic and authoritarian male leaders play a central role. Fundamentalist movements are highly dependent on their charismatic leader to break open the religious tradition for his followers, plumbing its richness to find a basis for group mobilization and activism. It is he who reads the signs of the times, interprets the will of God and devises a general plan of action. The charismatic leader speaks for an angry God who calls true believers to uncommon feats of devotion and self-sacrifice in the battle against evil. As fundamentalist organizations develop over time, the charismatic leader may become somewhat aloof from day-to-day planning and the setting of policy, but his broadsides against rival religious leaders or political figures continue to provide a powerful impetus for group action. When a specific operation involves a group in illegal activities, or even in activities forbidden by religious law and by religious leaders of the group, the charismatic leader may reject responsibility for the operation. In the case of certain terrorist acts conducted by young radicals affiliated with Hezbollah (Party of God) in Lebanon, for example, the movement's religious authorities, Muslim scholars such as the fiery preacher Sheik Muhammad Hosein Fadlallah, were ultimately unable to control the furies their preaching unleashed. To take another example, few question the fact that Sheik Rahman preached a radical fundamentalist message to worshippers in his mosques in Egypt and New Jersey; controversy surrounds, instead, his claim that he should not be held responsible for the illegal actions of zealous young men who sought to give concrete expression, via the bombing of public sites in New York City, to his diatribes against the Mubarak regime and its supporters.

At the same time that fundamentalists envy and resent modernity, they shrewdly exploit its processes and instrumentalities. Ayatollah Khomeini changed the course of Iranian history when cassette tapes of his sermons were smuggled into the country during the last days of Muhammad Reza Shah Pahlavi (1941–79). Shiism was itself transformed in the ensuing revolution. Several of the Eastern fundamentalistlike movements that arose during or immediately after the colonial period consciously imitated the West. Hindu groups under the raj, for example, adopted Western organizational models, a process that transformed the structures of traditional religion. As religion historian

Daniel Gold notes: "Where once people found religious authority in their family priest or a lineage of gurus, they may now find it in a formalized organizational hierarchy....If fundamentalist religion implies a resolute religious reaction to forces of modernity, then fundamentalist Hinduism is necessarily organized Hinduism."

Serving the Disadvantaged

The failed policies of secular regimes and the unpopular or esoteric teachings of religious liberals and modernists have given fundamentalisms an additional boost. Perhaps even more important in explaining fundamentalisms' popular appeal is their consistent service to people in need. Fundamentalist social networks, alternate institutions and welfare programs are a way of recruiting members, of building sympathy in the larger community and of fighting back against godless regimes. The Muslim Brotherhood established a network of social-service institutions crisscrossing Egypt. These have served as a safety net of sorts for thousands of displaced migrants to Cairo and other cities. Originally conceived as Hasan al-Banna's response to timid moral leadership on the part of the ulema, these agencies with their social outreach have given the Muslim Brotherhood access to the mainstream of Egyptian life, even as it has spawned radical splinter groups which eschew conventional and gradualist means of social transformation. "The dynamism of the spirit of Islamization," writes Middle East historian John O. Voll, "is reflected in the growing numbers of people involved in social and political activism of a nonmilitant style [in Egypt]."

Fundamentalist institutions also offer an extraordinary religious canopy under which people can congregate. Thus social agencies have been breeding grounds not only for radical activists but more often for fundamentalist missionaries working within Sikhism, Christianity, Islam, or within Habad, a distinctive sect within ultra-Orthodox Judaism.

As fundamentalisms diversify, in other words, they are themselves broadened and deepened as social movements.

A countervailing tendency operates when fundamentalist social institutions function as "worlds within the world," controlled environments in which the fundamentalist plan is realized in microcosm. Ultra-Orthodox Jews in Israel—also known as *haredim,* for their attitude of anxiety in the face of imminent divine judgment—send their sons to the particular sect's yeshiva, or religious academy, for full-time study of Jewish texts, law and lore. The "yeshiva world" is all-encompassing; devotion to its ritualized forms of study exempts men from service in the Israeli army and requires women also to study in their own academies or, more commonly, to support the large families that they produce.

This spectrum of social functions is well represented within North American Christian fundamentalism, a multi-generational phenomenon which has enjoyed ample time to diversify. Incipient fundamentalists formed institutions in the Depression days of the 1930s that served thousands of alienated Americans "on the margins"—economically, socially, culturally, emotionally. Thousands of independent fundamentalist churches sprang up in rural and urban areas and sponsored group activities for every night of the week. Meanwhile, the broad-based appeal of Charles E. Fuller's old-fashioned revival hour in the early 1940s was revealed in "the many letters he had received from heartbroken, heart-hungry humanity, contemplating suicide," for whom his re-assuring message of purpose and hope made a difference. Professor Ammerman summarizes the import of these various networks, agencies and institutions: "To become a fundamentalist was to join a group—a local, visible, supportive community. Living in a hostile world required nothing less."

Another brand of alternate institution began to thrive in the "hostile world" of the 1960s and 1970s, the Christian school. Christian academies and day schools have tripled in number during the past 20 years. They attempt to provide a "total world," encompassing every aspect of students' lives, with a pedagogy and curriculum rooted in the "Christian" worldview: fundamentalist history is *His* story; fundamentalist math, an entrée to the ordered and dependable processes of creation; fundamentalist science, a lens by which to view an enchanted universe sustained at every moment by divine providence. Although the primary goal of these academies is to train Christian preachers and missionaries, many of their graduates will matriculate at one of the new Christian universities and colleges that are preparing students for entry into the mainstream of American life.

Televangelism

Many of the traits associated with fundamentalism—the envy of the modern, the tendency to foster a sense of crisis and urgency, the flair for the dramatic and symbolic act—attracted fundamentalists to the mass media. They not only understood the media but manipulated them effectively. Increasingly, as the twentieth century wore on, the television set (or radio) rather than the local synagogue, church or mosque was the center for the celebration, elaboration and reinforcement of religious and communal identity.

Modern media are ideal for those who wish to reach the outsider, the marginalized. Through the media, the margin may become the center, or one of many centers. North and South American Christian televangelism (and mass outdoor rallies by televangelists promoted on the airwaves) are the obvious examples of the canny use of communications technology. Perhaps more striking are the unfamiliar examples, such as the skillful use of the media and the lavish productions at the Pathum Thani headquarters of the Wat Dhammakaya in Thailand. This Buddhist sect is the fastest-growing religious movement in Thailand, with militant, fundamentalistlike tendencies. Its broad-based popular support, according to Professor Swearer, "stems from an astute [media] packaging of a fundamentalistic form of Thai Buddhism that offers a way of embracing a secularized modern life-style while retaining the communal identity once offered by traditional Buddhism—all the while maintaining that it is 'authentic' or 'true' Buddhism, in contrast to its

Police drive back some of the 6,000 ultra-Orthodox Jews of Jerusalem's Mea Shearim neighborhood who protest the opening of a new road in October 1991.

Reuters/Bettmann

competitors." Similarly, members of Israel's Gush Emunim "staged" the planting of settlements in the territories for the benefit of the Israeli media, who were enthralled by the Gush theatrics. For their part, the religiously motivated settlers wished to convince fence-sitting Israelis of the wisdom of the occupation. To take a final example, Deiros's description of fundamentalism as an "impulse" within Latin American evangelicalism evokes the way in which fundamentalism is spread through media images and sound bites, as well as through the organizations and structures of a mass movement.

In Summary

Fundamentalisms package traditional religion in modern wrappings that attract people from very different social classes and educational backgrounds. When they are most successful, fundamentalisms occupy a niche in the social ecology of the nation or region; that is, they plant roots in the cultural soil and become a part of the fabric of everyday life. Policymakers who oppose or seek to diminish the influence of fundamentalisms as a religious and political expression would do well to recognize the myriad ways in which they reflect the soul of a people. No less important, however, they should be aware of the ways in which Islamic or Christian or Jewish or Hindu politics may also distort a people's deepest religious values and cultural identity.

3

The Impact of Fundamentalisms

The fundamentalist movements surveyed here have originated in radically different socioeconomic and political contexts. Some contend against secular states; others form majorities or minorities within a sectarian state. The movements can be differentiated by the sacred texts and traditions to which they turn for guidance, by their doctrines and their gods, and by their various political alliances. Finally, each movement is a minority within the larger religious tradition from which it has emerged. And, as the directors of The Fundamentalism Project noted:

> The images of violence on the West Bank and Gaza, of revolution in the streets of Iran, of assassinations and massacres in the Punjab, are misleading if they are not balanced with images of moderate Sikhs eschewing violence and condemning extremism, of Shiite refugees pinned helplessly in the Lebanese crossfire, and of observant Jews in Israel calling for negotiations with Palestinian Arabs…. Nor is truth served if fundamentalists are portrayed, in headlines or studies, as in every case committed to violence, as obstructionists, as unthinking foes of progress, or as inherently representative of a regressive trend in religion and in human civilization.

Yet these disparate movements seem to share certain "family resemblances" that help explain how fundamentalist religion and politics are joined in the late twentieth century. As has been shown, fundamentalisms thrive when and where masses in formerly traditional societies experience dislocation as a result of rapid and uneven modernization; when social, economic and cultural patterns change haphazardly; when educational and social-welfare systems fail their students and clients. In such times of crisis, people are needy in a particular way. Their hunger for material goods and political autonomy is matched by a thirst for spiritual reassurance and fulfillment.

Religion, presented as an encompassing way of life, suggests itself as the bearer of the power to meet these needs. It establishes and enforces codes of behavior, binding together people who share an experience of oppression or dislocation and sending them forth into the laboratories and schools and political parties and militias in order to secure and expand the borders of the sacred community. Unlike their nonfundamentalist coreligionists, fundamentalists demand that the codes of behavior be applied not only to family life and interpersonal relations but to political organizations and international economies as well. Fundamentalists strive for comprehensive measures because they have learned that traditional life based in the home, school, village or tribe is not sufficient to ward off the invasive colonizing "other." The religious community must therefore reject artificial distinctions between "private" and "public" realms.

At once defenders and constructors of a world built on religious fundamentals, true believers in the late twentieth century continually bump up against nonbelievers or lukewarm believers who dwell in the neighboring nation or town, or even in the home community or the nuclear family. Life for fundamentalists, as for most people, is an endless process of negotiation and compromise. Yet this situation frustrates those who believe they possess the ultimate truth about reality and who embrace unambiguous norms for righteous living based on that truth. Since fundamentalists are anxious to order society on that basis, they may seek control over people with whom they disagree. The irony is that the de facto pluralism of most societies today—the coexistence within geographic borders of different ethnic and/or religious groups, each with its own claim to autonomy—limits the ability of any one minority to impose its will upon the whole. And in most cases, religious fundamentalists find themselves in the minority.

Nonetheless, their religion gives this particular minority a decided advantage by providing a cause whose importance outweighs the value of the believer's life or liberty. Religious rituals, such as the self-flagellation of Shiites commemorating Ashura (the day of the martyrdom of Imam Husein, grandson of the Prophet) or the prayers of Operation Rescue members lying in a fetal position blocking the doors of American abortion clinics, locate the believer in a sacred cosmos that rewards martyrdom or imprisonment in the service of God. Less sensational but no less heroic are the daily self-sacrifices of fundamentalists who seek to remake the world.

Immortality and Compassion

Heroism and self-sacrifice, fundamentalist-style, reflect a belief (not unique to fundamentalists) in the possibility of personal or collective immortality. The expectation of an afterlife, although understood in very different ways by the religious groups, gives fundamentalist leaders an important psychological advantage in mobilizing people for dangerous assignments and in retaining them as active members in the long-term operations of a movement. As Benedict Anderson, professor of international relations at Cornell University, has observed, there is no "Tomb of the Unknown Marxist" or memorial for fallen liberals, for neither Marxism nor liberalism are much concerned with death and immortality.

The religious imagination of fundamentalists is also a vision of mercy. Compassion for the suffering of others finds concrete expression in the thousands of health-care clinics, orphanages, hospitals, schools, and service agencies sponsored by fundamentalist movements or individuals around the world. The good done by these institutions is at least as important in winning recruits for the cause as are the rallies and riots. In both cases, the success of fundamentalisms stands as an indictment of the weaknesses of secular systems in providing for human psychological and social needs.

Time spent observing their secular opponents at close range enables fundamentalists to imitate the ways and adopt the means of the enemy: fundamentalists are increasingly at ease in parliaments and press conferences, and are adept at mass-mail lobbying and computer-driven technologies. Politics informed by fundamentalist religion is in many ways like "politics-as-usual": in all but the most oppressive dictatorships, compromise and negotiation are its lifeblood, and adaptation to changing political realities is its mode of response.

But fundamentalist politics also proceeds according to the dictates of particular organizations and ideologies. Fundamentalists may attempt, as the Islamists did for a time in Algeria, to overcome or minimize the reluctance of voters by projecting an image of moderation. But they may also follow a strategy of polarization designed to provoke their opponents and scandalize the world, thereby hoping to tap xenophobic energies of the masses and to awaken previously politically somnolent sympathizers.

While zeal and increasing political sophistication have carried fundamentalist groups to power or to the brink of power in several nations, the fundamentalists have seldom proven themselves capable of actually governing effectively. One economist has described the economic policies of the BJP, India's Hindu party, as "changing, vague and incoherent." The BJP rejects the "foreign" influences of Islam, Christianity, capitalism and socialism alike as failed remedies for India's deep-rooted social and economic problems, but has posed no viable alternative. To varying degrees the same can be said of Islamic, Jewish, Christian, Sikh and Buddhist fundamentalists: they have proven themselves skilled at discerning the problems of society and naming the perpetrators, but they have been far less impressive in posing workable solutions.

Fundamentalists thus find it difficult to govern without resorting to the services of professional politicians and nonfundamentalist allies. Men and women motivated primarily—if not exclusively—by religious considerations are caught in a dilemma when they attempt to create the world they have imagined. Reliance on sympathizers and advisers from outside the inner circle can lead quickly to the politics of compromise and the distillation of the fundamentalist sociomoral message. Conversely, rule by political or military professionals can lead to a despotic hardening of fundamentalist laws as a justification for the imposition of a police state.

Strange Bedfellows

Another way of negotiating political influence finds fundamentalist leaders and secular politicians entering tacitly or openly into a mutually beneficial alliance to advance shared temporal goals. Fundamentalist leaders are willing to be carried along on a wave of socioeconomic or purely political resentment, while secular politicians provide financial and political support for the religious "pioneers" who will say and do things that a "mainstream" politician studiously avoids. In the 1980s the Christian Right in the United States was co-opted and used by a powerful and sophisticated secular political group—the ultra-conservative wing of the Republican party. Similarly, Jewish fundamentalists proved to be useful agents of an expansionist policy of a secular government and Israelis who did not necessarily share the religious doctrine or ideology of the radicals.

These patterns may change, however, as fundamentalists gain more experience in playing the political game on their own terms. The Christian Right, in the aftermath of the 1992

Republican National Convention in Houston, Texas, and the ensuing U.S. presidential election, for example, became an impressive and highly effective grass-roots political movement with a very bright future. Islamic fundamentalist movements have vied or are vying for political power in Algeria, Pakistan, Egypt, Lebanon, Nigeria and Jordan, among other countries. These movements have relied on diverse strategies to make an impact on different levels of political society. Some formed political parties to work within the confines of the social contract established by the regime in power. "Islamization" was attempted both through alliances with the ruler (as in Pakistan under President Zia ul-Haq, 1978–88) and through initial moves toward democratic reform, as in Egypt and Algeria. Islamic groups benefited in the short term, but their political forays also exposed flaws in the fundamentalist program to translate religious law and Quranic precept into a coherent modern political ideology capable of inspiring effective solutions for difficult problems. Islam itself, like Christianity and Judaism, often seemed diminished by its direct politicalization.

The Christian Right in the United States

"Wishful thinking" is perhaps the best way to characterize the confident predictions of the liberal American press and television media who, after President George Bush's defeat in his 1992 bid for reelection, pronounced postmortems not only over the political corpse of the one-term Texan from Maine, but also over the still-warm body of the Religious Right. Conservative Protestant evangelicals, supported by the Roman Catholic conservative Patrick J. Buchanan, Bush's opponent in the primaries, had been perhaps the most visible, vocal and strident bloc at the Republican National Convention—and had helped shape the tone and content of the convention, as well as the party platform on which Bush was to run (and which he attempted to ignore during the campaign). The Christian Right was thus a handy scapegoat when Bush lost. Conventional wisdom held that the platform, with its homophobic rhetoric and strict restrictions against abortion, was too far to the right for the American electorate and, along with Buchanan's much-discussed "we are in a culture war" speech invoking the language of a religious crusade, had alienated moderate conservatives within the party.

Exhibiting something of the same thinly disguised glee and self-satisfaction with which they had reported the decline and disbanding of the fundamentalist Rev. Jerry Falwell's political coalition, the Moral Majority, in 1989, the secular media predicted that televangelist Pat Robertson's Christian Coalition had seen its last days as an effective force in American political life. On the morning after the election results were posted, NBC-TV *Today* cohost Bryant Gumbel asked Robertson whether the vast majority of voters hadn't found the mixing of politics and fundamentalist religion distasteful. Hadn't the "traditional family values" rhetoric backfired, thereby discrediting the Christian activists? In hoping to play a more decisive role in political power-brokering than they had enjoyed in the Reagan years (1981–89), when they had been kept in their corner by their more politically sophisticated secular neoconservative coalition-partners, hadn't the heirs of the Moral Majority overplayed their hand?

No, Robertson replied vigorously, the American public had not rejected traditional family values or Christian politicians; they had rejected the failing economy and an Administration that seemed incapable of reinvigorating it. Rather than abandoning the Republican party, however, the Christian Right had supported Bush impressively, Robertson claimed, preventing the President from losing in a landslide. On subsequent television and radio programs, Bay Buchanan, Patrick's sister and campaign manager, amplified this "spin" on the election results: far from being defeated, she proclaimed, the Christian Right was ahead of schedule in its attempt to build a viable political bloc within the Republican party. Having won control of the national platform committee four years earlier than anticipated, they were now positioning their candidates for state and local races.

From the evidence that has accumulated since the election, it appears that Robertson and the Buchanans were better spin doctors than Gumbel. Two Republican senators were so alarmed by the surprising persistence of the Religious Right that they formed a committee to counter and diminish its influence within the Republican party. That influence was documented in the aftermath of the election, as pollsters and political scientists revised the earlier (under)estimates of evangelical voter turnout for the GOP. (This abbreviation of Grand Old Party is now taken to stand for God's Own Party by pundits.) Exit polls conducted by a consortium of four television networks estimated that "born-again" Christians, among whom Bush won easily, constituted 17 percent of the electorate; a team of moderate evangelical political scientists, including Lyman A. Kellstedt of Wheaton College and Corwin E. Smidt of Calvin College, argue that this number swells to 25 percent when one includes voters within the "broad evangelical tradition"—Missouri Synod Lutherans, conservative Presbyterians, and nondenominational evangelicals ("perhaps the most politicized sector of conservative Protestantism, constituting about 4 percent of the electorate"). The exit-poll analysts concluded that, far from driving nonfundamentalist voters away, the GOP hardline stance on abortion, gay rights and other social issues "had appeal even outside the evangelical camp, but could not overcome disenchantment with Bush's economic mismanagement."

Fundamentalist Targets: Gay Rights and Abortion

Revitalized by victories in the state elections of 1992, the Christian Right waged its side of the culture war with renewed vigor and a clearer sense of purpose in 1993. The question of gay rights was a battleground. Prominent among the 1992 victories was the passing of Colorado's Amendment 2, which bans local laws barring discrimination against homosexuals. The Christian Coalition, drawing on its extensive grass roots—the organization claims 350,000 national members in 600 county chapters—plans similar measures for California, Idaho, Missouri, Oregon, Ohio and Washington as part of an overall "no special rights for homosexuals" strategy. In April 1993, the Christian Coalition enlisted the help of the Roman Catholic Archdiocese of New York in distributing voter guides for the school-board elections and opposing the Rainbow Curriculum, a controversial program designed to foster tolerance, which included lessons appearing to endorse homosexual relationships (e.g.,"Daddy's Roommate," "Heather has Two Mommies," and "Gloria Goes to Gay Pride"). In this effort, Robertson's organization joined forces with the Christian Action Network, an outgrowth of the Moral Majority, which claims 67,000 active contributors and 200,000 supporters. Meanwhile, the California-based Traditional Values Coalition, led by the Reverend Lou Sheldon, opened an office in Minneapolis, Minn., to direct a campaign against antidiscrimination laws protecting homosexuals in Minnesota; and the Oregon Citizens Alliance, led by Lon Mabon, changed the wording but not the intent of a narrowly defeated 1992 initiative to forbid minority status to homosexuals and the use of tax monies to promote or express approval of homosexuality.

Abortion remained a hotly contested social issue, with extremists on both sides. Too much is at stake here, so the reasoning went, for Americans to take refuge in moderation. For pro-lifers, the protection of human (including fetal) life is a fundamental obligation regarding which there can be no compromise or middle ground; for pro-choice advocates, the reproductive freedom of women is the predominant value. In 1993 antiabortion radicals continued to steal the headlines from the larger and tactically more moderate pro-life movement. The most publicized and troubling event was the March 10 assassination of David Gunn, a 47-year-old doctor, by a protester at an abortion clinic in Pensacola, Fla.

In the courts, Christian activists scored triumphs on the

question of school prayer and religious freedom, the most significant of which was a Supreme Court refusal to consider, much less overturn, a Texas case allowing student-initiated prayer during public-school graduation ceremonies. Robertson's American Center for Law and Justice had promoted the Texas ruling in response to an earlier Supreme Court case prohibiting as unconstitutional state-sponsored prayers at such events.

Clearly, the Christian Right emerged from the 1992 elections with far brighter prospects than outsiders (and even some insiders) might have conceded to it after the Republican convention. What set of circumstances accounts for the renewed fortunes of the religious activists?

Focus on Grass-Roots Politics

First, there is the rise of what might be called "board fundamentalism." Learning its lessons from the experience of Falwell's Moral Majority, which concentrated its resources and energies on Washington in the attempt to become a congressional lobby and pressure group, the new generation (Ralph Reed, the director of the Christian Coalition, is in his mid-thirties) of Christian activists has turned attention to hundreds of local communities around the nation. Grass-roots politics, based on the training of Christian candidates for local school boards, hospital and college boards and state assemblies, has replaced, or perhaps complemented, the erstwhile focus on the federal government. In the smaller settings, where decisions are taken that directly affect the allocation of funds and the implementation of laws and policies, fundamentalists and conservative evangelicals are opposing the teaching of evolution, attempting to stem the tide of pornography and sexual license, and fighting back against "liberal" medical ethics. That they are doing so now without resorting to running "stealth candidates," who hide their religiopolitical affiliations, is an indication of their growing strength and self-confidence. The new emphasis on grass-roots politics does not preclude an eventual return to the national limelight; indeed, the Christian activists now recognize that local activism is the necessary prerequisite for such a return.

A second recent development is the deliberate attempt of Christian conservatives to avoid the infighting and hairsplitting that have hampered their political efforts in the past and to forge broad alliances across theological and denominational lines—fundamentalists (like Falwell) with Pentecostals (like Robertson), conservative evangelicals with conservative Catholics, and occasionally, Orthodox Jews with any or all of the above. The theological orientation and heritage of Pentecostals is different from that of fundamentalists. The Pentecostal view of history as an unfolding and dynamic process is much more fluid than the fundamentalists' sense that God has foreordained a precise beginning, middle and (approaching) end to human affairs. Pentecostals believe that the Bible is the true Word of God, but they remain open to the leading of the Holy Spirit. Fundamentalists are uncomfortable with the open-ended character of Pentecostalism and feel that the Bible alone is sufficient in guiding Christian moral, religious and political action. Falwell did not support Robertson's run for the presidency in 1988, despite their similar calls for a return to traditional moral values: a fundamentalist finds it difficult to entrust the future to anyone who is waiting for a new whisper of revelation from the Lord.

Yet Falwell and Robertson stood side by side in the 1992 campaign, increasingly acknowledged their common evangelical heritage and voiced essentially the same moral critique of American secular humanism and materialism. Today, their respective television ministries reinforce one another and contribute in a powerful way to the momentum of fundamentalistlike social movements in the United States. Indeed, the most prominent leaders of the Christian Right seem to have taken to heart Jesus' adage in the New Testament: "Who is not against us is with us."

Even the radical antiabortionist Randall Terry, the Christian fundamentalist founder of Operation Rescue, shares the larger religiopolitical vision of Falwell and Robertson: he sees Operation Rescue and the campaign against abortion as but the first step in returning America to its Christian roots and destiny. In "The Glory and the Power," a recent television documentary, Terry explains:

> You know, I am an evangelist!... I've stood on street corners and said, 'Excuse me, everyone, can I have your attention?' And I preach the gospel of the living God to them! 'Jesus Christ died for your sins. He rose from the dead on the third day and you can believe in Him and be forgiven!' But where we part company with some wings of the church, the separatist wing of the church, is that they think that is it! That is the sum total of our duty as Christians to this generation. And I reject that!

Finally, the current sociopolitical climate in the United States almost necessitates the taking of sides and accelerates the erosion of any middle ground. The conceit that Americans are trapped in a clash of cultures with irreconcilable worldviews inevitably raises the profile of militants, who thrive on the crisis mentality. The distance between "culture war" and "conspiracy theory" is not great; and the notion of a conspiracy of liberal and secular agents bent on undermining the traditional cultural values and civil institutions of America is grist for the fundamentalist mill. Pat Robertson was marketing a grand conspiracy theory even in the latter days of the Bush Administration, with his adroit fusing of Christian apocalyptic themes and a rigorous moral critique of contemporary American society. As Soviet communism waned, he perceived a new enemy, a coming global threat of one-worldism inspired by New Age philosophy that he exposed in his 1991 best-seller, *The New World Order:*

> A single thread runs from the White House to the State Department to the Council on Foreign Relations to the Trilateral Commission to secret societies to extreme New Agers. There must be a new world order. It must eliminate national sovereignty. There must be world government, a world police force, world courts, world banking and currency, and a world elite in charge of it all. To some there must be a complete

redistribution of wealth; to others there must be an elimination of Christianity; to some extreme New Agers there must be the deaths of 2 or 3 billion people in the Third World by the end of this decade.

By the inner logic of this approach, the election of Bill Clinton as President in 1992 was perhaps the best thing that could have happened for the Christian Right (better, in fact, than if a born-again fundamentalist had won and found himself confronted with the challenge of actually governing). Jim Smith of the Southern Baptist Christian Life Commission announced that the election of Clinton would reveal the sordid face of true liberalism and thereby "wake folks up" to the threat posed by the enemy. Martin Mawyer, head of the Christian Action Network, offered an example of the "Clinton backlash" theory in predicting that the National Endowment for the Arts, beleaguered under a Republican President for its "trashy art," will face even stiffer Republican congressional opposition under a Clinton appointee.

In the Clinton era, the Christian Right is taking a calculated risk that most Americans will be turned off by the excesses of unvarnished liberalism run amok. Margaret O'Brien Steinfels, editor of the moderate-to-liberal American Catholic magazine *Commonweal,* complained about the smug complacency and glib secularism of her otherwise beloved *New York Times,* which exhibited, she charged, traces of anti-Catholicism in its coverage of the controversy over the Rainbow Curriculum. She excoriated *The Times* for its inattention to reasonable objections raised by parents who preferred not to have their first graders taught that same-sex couples are no different than normal families; for its "very partial if not highly distorted" portrayal of the kind of people opposed to the curriculum; and for the reporters' inability to treat religious objections to homosexuality or homosexual conduct as other than bigotry. The opponents, Steinfels noted, included Catholics, Orthodox Jews, African American Protestants and Hispanics, "all of whom were dismissed as members of the Religious Right by *The Times.*"

This is precisely the type of consternation that the Christian Right expects the new liberalism to provoke, not only in conservatives but in moderates. In the present situation, the new generation of Christian activists believes, there is no place for moderation. And, ironically, it is this belief which is at the heart of their great optimism.

Crackdown on Fundamentalists in Egypt and Algeria

In Egypt and Algeria, religious fundamentalism is different in form and impact, not only because Islam, rather than Christianity, is the host religion of the fundamentalists, but because the internal political and cultural conditions in Egypt and Algeria, on the one hand, and the United States on the other, are so different. America's well-developed civil society—strong, independent voluntary associations, labor unions, a free press and other institutions that stand between the government and the citizen—presents a political environment in which fundamentalists are encouraged to play by the rules of the democratic game and reap the rewards or suffer the consequences.

In Algeria and Egypt, each with its own history of one-party rule and an overbearing military presence in government, Muslim fundamentalists were caught in the contradictions of political systems that promised liberalization and the growth of civil society but were not ready to deliver on the promises. Islamists who vied for power legally were either directly rebuked when they succeeded at the democratic game (Algeria) or restricted and co-opted by an all-powerful central government (Egypt).

In 1992 the Islamic Salvation Front (FIS)* was poised to assume a commanding majority in the Algerian parliament before President Chadli Benjedid of the ruling National Liberation Front (FLN)* resigned on January 11, thereby delivering the government into the hands of the military and ending Algeria's three-year experiment in democracy.

By winning 188 of 231 seats contested in December 1991 in the first free national legislative elections since Algeria

Islamic fundamentalists' protests against one-party rule of President Chadli Benjedid were met by tanks in 1988. Less than three years later, local democratic elections were held, but in January 1992 Algeria reverted to military rule.

gained its independence from France in 1962, the Islamists surprised even the most pessimistic of their secular opponents, none of whom had predicted that they would garner more than one third of the popular vote. Exploiting widespread disgust with the FLN, the Socialist party that has controlled Algeria for some 30 years despite a record of inefficiency and corruption, the Islamists mobilized the disgruntled and the zealous alike, including thousands of veiled Algerian women clad in traditional Islamic garb.

The government version of events leading up to the December 1991 election held that the Islamists would falter as a result of voter dissatisfaction with their incompetent administration of the municipalities they had won in the June 1990 local elections. Yet the FIS was better organized and more popular than the other alternatives to the ruling party, including the Front for Socialist Forces, which took a mere 25 seats in the December voting. Thus the establishment found itself in a no-win situation in the wake of this first round of elections. With more than 200 additional seats in parliament to be decided in the January 16 election, the Islamists were only 28 seats short of a simple majority, and well within reach of the two-thirds majority that would allow them to rewrite Algeria's constitution on the model of an Islamic republic. A government-appointed Constitutional Council proceeded to investigate "voting irregularities" involving at least 70 of the National People's Assembly seats won by the FIS. The government also launched a campaign to arouse antifundamentalist Algerians, 200,000 of whom staged massive protests in the weeks following the election. But this strategy proved futile and short-lived. In his statement of resignation, Benjedid bemoaned the fact that the democratization process he had inaugurated in 1988 (under intense pressure) had become "riddled with irregularities and cannot be continued safely"— a phrasing that suggested, at the very least, an imperfect understanding of what genuine democratization is all about. Tanks and armored vehicles took up positions around government buildings, television and radio stations, and telephone exchanges, in order, as Prime Minister Sid Ahmed Ghozali explained, "to protect public security" in the wake of Benjedid's resignation. Three days later a State Security Panel composed of military and civilian leaders canceled the second round of elections and announced the creation of a five-man body, the Council of State, to rule the country until December 1993. Described as a "junta" by FIS spokesmen, this ruling body was headed by a founding member of the FLN.

A thoroughgoing crackdown on the FIS followed, with the arrests of hundreds of Islamists. The ruling body banned rallies and other political activities at mosques, a move widely interpreted as intended to taunt and provoke the poor and jobless young men who constituted the inner cell of FIS supporters.

In covering these developments in Algeria, the Western media reflected a bias against the FIS. Most reporters assumed that no rational voter would choose the FIS, an Islamic party, on its own merits, only if coerced or deceived. For who would choose a party that wished to impose "the chilling penal law known as Sharia *[sic]*"? Evidently lost on the *Time* reporter who wrote those words was the fact that the penal code, including the *hudud* punishments for adultery, theft and other crimes, comprises only a small portion of the Sharia. Nor was it inevitable that the Algerian Islamists would exercise power in this way. American University political scientist Amos Perlmutter, writing in the editorial section of *The Washington Post*, thought that it was inevitable. All fundamentalist "impact" is the same, he argued; there are no viable distinctions to be made between Islamic movements around the world, for "Islamic fundamentalism of the Sunni or Shia variety in Iran, Iraq, Egypt, Jordan, the West Bank and Gaza, the Maghreb and also Algeria is not merely resistant to democracy but wholly contemptuous of and hostile to the entire democratic political culture….[It] is an aggressive revolutionary movement as militant and violent as the Bolshevik, Fascist and Nazi movements of the past." A failure to do a case-by-case analysis leads to such lumping together of peoples and movements, and Perlmutter tipped his hand by asserting in the same editorial that the world's 800 million Muslims should be viewed as one monolithic force. "The issue is not democracy but the true nature of Islam," he wrote. "Is Islam, fundamentalist or otherwise, compatible with liberal, human-rights-oriented Western-style representative democracy? The answer is an emphatic 'no.'"

Islam and Democracy

The manifestations of Islamic fundamentalism in the Sudan and in Iran, regimes comparable in their disregard for Western standards of human rights, were echoed in the chant of 100,000 Algerians at a stadium rally on election eve—"We recognize no constitution and no laws but the laws of God and Islam"—and the call for the veiling of women and their retreat from the workplace. While the Algerian supporters of the FIS were motivated more by a passion for Islam than for democracy, a long-term alliance between the two is possible. The Quran and the Sharia provide a sociomoral framework rather than a detailed blueprint for political order and allow a degree of adaptation and flexibility in state-building, as the history of Islam demonstrates. The quest for sovereignty may result in a gradual process of incorporation and "Islamization" of Western structures and mechanisms, including mass participation in democratic procedures. Indeed, this has been the pattern followed in the Islamists' appropriation of Western science and technology, which they describe as an act of "repossession."

Abdelkader Hachani, the acting head of the FIS before his arrest on January 22, 1992, insisted that an Algerian Islamic government will be different from theocracy in Iran or military rule in Sudan. "We guarantee freedom of opinion in Algeria. Our purpose is to persuade, not to oblige, people into doing what we say. We have won control of over 800 municipalities in elections of over a year ago. We have a record of tolerance that no one can deny. This is the essence of Islam." Considering the alternatives to Islamic rule in Algeria, namely, a martial-law regime or more of the same governmental mismanagement that led to a 100 percent inflation rate and a 25 percent unemployment rate, one can only wonder at the Western media's rush to judgment.

Muslim fundamentalists' desire to establish the Sharia as the explicit, comprehensive and exclusive legal basis for society is a goal not shared by the vast majority of Muslims. Nor does their general commitment to implement Islamic law across the board lead all fundamentalists down the same path. Like any complex legal code developed over time, the Sharia permits many interpretations and diverse applications.

University of Khartoum professor Akmed An Naim, a leader of an Islamic reform movement in the Sudan called the Republican Brothers, has argued that a "fundamentalist" retrieval of Islamic law may be reconcilable with Western notions of human rights in civil society. Imprisoned without charge in 1984 by then Sudanese President Jafar Muhammad Numayri, a self-proclaimed fundamentalist, An Naim protested that Numayri's brand of Islamic fundamentalism, shared by other Islamic radicals in the Middle East, was a mistaken attempt to impose the Sharia as an antidote to Western neocolonialism and cultural domination. He argued that the elements of Sharia invoked by Numayri (and Khomeini)—the prescriptions revealed to Muhammad in Medina dealing with penal law, civil liberties, and the treatment of minorities and women—promoted a "historically dated Islamic self-identity that needs to be reformed." Islamic economic and social justice and the exercise of legitimate political power depend upon the retrieval of the teachings of the Prophet in Mecca, which provide, in An Naim's judgment, "the moral and ethical foundation" of the tradition. "The Medina message is not the fundamental, universal, eternal message of Islam. That founding message is from Mecca," he writes. "This counterabrogation (of the Medina code) will result in the total conciliation between Islamic law and the modern development of human rights and civil liberties."

Islamic Law and Government

Rare is the disputant in such a conflict who does not claim to be upholding "the fundamentals." Rather, the battle is often over what they are, where they are to be found, how and by whom they are to be interpreted. In demanding the retrieval of the Mecca prophecy, An Naim concludes, "we [Republican Brothers] are the *superfundamentalists.*" The possibility of a "progressive" fundamentalist government does not ensure, of course, the existence of one. If the fundamentalists do win in Algeria (as they likely will, sooner or later, despite the military repression), they may or may not behave in accord with the best interests either of the West or the Algerian people. But there is more than one way to implement Islamic law. The situation may allow, or necessitate, the kind of shrewd compromise with secular governments and economies that has characterized the "conservative fundamentalist" monarchy in Saudi Arabia (which is increasingly opposed by homegrown radical fundamentalists, incited by the presence of Christian and Jewish soldiers in the Muslim Holy Land during the Persian Gulf crisis). Or the situation in Algeria may eventually approximate that in Egypt, where lip service, public ceremony, co-opted senior ulema, and occasional deferential rulings of government (that is, secular) courts take the place of the actual implementation of Islamic law. Because either of these options stands a better chance of preventing large-scale North African emigration to Europe, they seem preferable to the importation of an Iranian-style theocracy, backed by Iranian-style patronage, to Algeria.

The comparison with Egypt is instructive, for Egypt had its own carefully calibrated response to the fundamentalist flare-up in Algeria. On December 26, 1991, a government court in Egypt, striving to uphold the regime's image as Defender of the Faith, sentenced the novelist Alla Hamed, his publisher and a book distributor, to eight years in prison. The court declared Hamed's 1988 novel, *A Distance in a Man's Mind*, to be blasphemous; the protagonist's suggestion that Islam is not "for all times and places," the court ruled, "threatened national unity and social peace." Encouraged by the government move, Al-Azhar University, the home of the Islamic establishment in Egypt, impounded a number of "forbidden" books on display at the Cairo International Book Fair, including a treatise on Islam and women's rights and a series of works on the relationship between Islam and politics by Egypt's senior security-court judge. Al-Azhar University's partner in defending the faith, President Mubarak, found this move a bit too extreme and intervened to lift the ban. Moderation rather than zeal in upholding Islam remains his policy.

By permitting a mild version of the "Islamic current" to

hold sway over public perceptions, however, the Egyptian government may well be aiding forces it seeks to suppress. Currently there are many levels and varieties of Islamic fundamentalism within Egypt's borders, and over the course of 40 years, since the Free Officers Movement that brought Gamal Abdel Nasser to power in 1954, the secularized military state has gradually perfected the art of constraining and containing Islamic militancy. In the Mubarak years, it has done so through a sophisticated policy that combines partial appeasement, assimilation, ruthless repression, constant surveillance and infiltration of radical cells, and control of the media. Nonetheless, the Islamic current endures, and the persistent but contained violence of the 1980s between state security forces and Muslim radicals has escalated in the 1990s to what both sides describe as a civil war. Dozens of radical fundamentalist groups and subgroups, including the one founded by Sheik Rahman, are waging a terrorist campaign against government officials. These clandestine radical splinter groups long ago rejected the moderation of the original fundamentalist movement, the Muslim Brotherhood, which today publishes a weekly newspaper, supports the Socialist Labor party, and has representatives in the Egyptian parliament. Young Islamic radicals have, meanwhile, taken over student organizations at most universities and constantly denounce what they perceive as the rampant corruption and inefficiency of the ruling party, which, they claim, long ago abandoned Islam.

Hindu Activists in India

A third pattern of fundamentalist-style political activism can be observed in India, a nation with stronger democratic traditions than Egypt or Algeria, with constitutional protection of individual rights in a pluralist society. Unlike the United States, however, India does not enjoy political stability as it struggles to realize its own expression of the nation-state, an imported concept. In a relatively unstable political environment, the forces that would redefine constitutional principles and the meaning of Indian citizenship prosper by capturing the religious imagination of the people.

Consider the extraordinary example of the caravan which embarked on a "sacred journey" in December 1991 from the southernmost tip of India to the city of Srinagar, some 1,500 miles away, on the northwestern border with Pakistan. In attendance were prominent members of the BJP, young Hindu activists of the paramilitary National Volunteer Corps, and agents of the World Hindu Council. Riding atop the lead Toyota, protected by a bulletproof plate, was the BJP president, Murli Manohar Joshi, a former professor of physics. He organized the caravan as a display of Indian national "unity."

The three groups believe that "Hinduness" is the authentic source of unity in the sprawling, multiethnic, multilingual, multireligious nation. India presently has a secular constitution, which favors no one religion but ensures the right of each group to worship as it pleases. The BJP and the paramilitary volunteer corps seek to alter that constitution by defining citizenship on the basis of Hinduness and to "Hinduize" all of India. The BJP anticipated that the three-month symbolic journey would scandalize not only the Sikh and Muslim separatists, but the secularists of the governing Congress party as well. The BJP president's vow to raise the saffron flag of the Hindu nation in the capital of the Muslim-dominated region of Kashmir was calculated to provoke Muslim riots and the consequent assertion of Indian state control over the contested region.

Much like the radical Jews among the settlers on the West Bank, the troika's cadres tried to induce a reluctant secular state to declare its true affinities; they reasoned that, when the issue was forced, the government would support their right to defend Hindu sovereignty in India. In such cases of fundamentalist provocation, any responsive action of a secular government to defend national integrity against a rebellious minority can be interpreted as an affirmation of a particular ethnoreligious identity for the entire nation. Funda-

**Punjab, India, February 19, 1992: Sikh voters are guarded against
threatened attacks by Sikh separatists on polling stations.**

mentalists provoke a crisis, identify their cause with the
nation's cause, and sit back to let the government do the en-
forcing. They draw strength from the absolutism implied in
the very concept of a sovereign nation, though they seek to
give a name to the principle of sovereignty, whether that
name be Rama, Allah, Yahweh or God.

The first violent reaction to the 1991–92 caravan came
when Sikh militants ambushed a bus carrying BJP followers
as it entered the northern Indian province of Punjab, where
Sikhs are concentrated. The gunmen, disguised as police officers, killed five people and wounded forty—the first act in
a cycle of violence that continued for days.

In 1983 members of a moderate Sikh political party
flocked to join the ranks of Jarnail Singh Bhindranwale, the
charismatic leader of the radical religious organization
Damdami Taksal. Because the moderates had failed to translate the demography of Punjab, which is heavily Sikh in
population, into permanent political power for the Sikh

61

majority, the radicals charged that the democratic option had only weakened and divided the Sikhs and extended rule by the Congress party. Even when a moderate Sikh government had ruled the Punjab, it formed alliances with other political parties, including Hindus. Bhindranwale took the road of violence. To the traditional symbols of the Sikh militants—the unshorn hair, short pants, and sword—he added the motorcycle and the revolver.

Thus the caravan that rolled through the Punjab in January 1992 was assured of provoking unrest. The sight of Hindu nationalists recalled the 1984 storming of the Sikh Golden Temple at Amritsar by Indian state security forces, an operation which claimed some 1,000 lives, made a martyr of Bhindranwale, and subsequently led to more Sikh deaths in Hindu-led riots that occurred after Prime Minister Indira Gandhi was assassinated by two vengeful Sikh bodyguards. Enraged by the return of Hindu militants, Sikh radicals raided the BJP caravan and shortly thereafter warned that they would kill anyone voting in the elections for parliament and the local legislatures scheduled for February 19, 1992. Despite the presence of a quarter of a million Indian state police officers and soldiers, the death threats kept away the vast majority (70 percent) of Punjab voters.

The Hindu caravan rolled on to Kashmir, where the Jammu and Kashmir Liberation Front has led Muslim separatists in their efforts to secede from India. In anticipation of the arrival of the caravan, Muslim militants bombed the regional police chief's office in Srinagar. BJP leaders called off plans to drive a large motorcade through the Vale of Kashmir. However, BJP President Joshi himself hoisted the Hindu flag in Srinagar's town square—although to do so he required the presence of tens of thousands of heavily armed troops and a total curfew in the area. Across the border in Pakistan, the Hindu caravan also had an unsettling impact. In February, with thousands of supporters trailing behind him, many of them members of the Jamaat-e-Islami, Amanullah Khan, Joshi's Pakistani counterpart, led a march toward Indian-controlled Kashmir. He was ready to die for Allah. "It's not important who leads, but I hope that I will get the first Indian bullet," he said. Pakistani police fired on the separatists trying to cross the border, and the then Pakistani prime minister, Nawaz Sharif, concerned about the possibility of a war with India, declared that Amanullah's action was "like throwing innocent people into the fire."

Sharif had won the October 1990 election by defeating the Pakistan People's party of Benazir Bhutto (she was later returned to power in the 1993 elections). The first head of government drawn from the middle class and not from the landowning aristocracy, Sharif tried to revive the national economy. His government removed most restrictions on currency as well as trade, and it began turning over many state-run companies and several banks to private owners. The Pakistani rupee quickly surpassed the Indian rupee in value. Yet the prime minister was caught between Pakistan's vocal and influential Muslim fundamentalists and the secular government of neighboring India. He referred to the Muslim marchers on India as "freedom fighters," but he halted the march, which angered the Islamic fundamentalists. Indeed, his policies seemed to reflect a mild case of schizophrenia. In 1991 he courted the fundamentalists by introducing a so-called Sharia bill in the wake of the Persian Gulf war. The bill satisfied the Islamic Democratic Alliance, but not the Jamaat-e-Islami party, which found it to be superficial and rejected it. With Pakistan under an American aid embargo, Sharif attempted to rehabilitate Pakistan's credibility with the West by abandoning the long-standing support of the Muslim fundamentalist fighters in neighboring Afghanistan.

What seemed schizophrenic was actually a carefully orchestrated policy designed to appease Muslims on domestic issues while applying the principles of realpolitik on the international front—a policy also followed by Arab leaders besieged by fundamentalist demands in Egypt and Jordan. Sharif's domestic policy seemed to backfire. "Islamic economics" had been a slogan rather than a serious policy in

Pakistan, but in 1992 the highest religious courts ordered the Pakistani government to suspend Western-style banking and abolish interest on bank deposits, loans, land acquisition, insurance and cooperative societies—moves that, if allowed to stand, would risk financial collapse, jeopardize international financial dealings, and thwart attempts to attract foreign investments. Islamic parties do not hold many seats in the National Assembly, but they form an important part of the governing coalition and wield enormous influence over the conservative and largely illiterate population. Such are the dynamics of fundamentalist impact in the region.

4

Interpretations of Fundamentalism

Many interpreters of fundamentalism emphasize its essentially negative character, noting that its impact has often been destructive. Thus the sociologist Majid Tehranian, among others, characterizes fundamentalism as essentially antisecularist, opposing the displacement of the sacred from the center to the periphery of society in countries like Iran and Guatemala and in regions like the Bible Belt in the United States. Similarly, Tehranian continues, an antielitist interpretation of fundamentalist movements points out that fundamentalism seems to appeal "primarily to the marginal classes, including the lower-middle-class urban populations (as in Guatemala), as well as the intelligentsia from the same social backgrounds (as in most of the Islamic world), suppressed ethnic or religious minorities (as the Shiites in Lebanon and Palestinians in Israel), and marginalized majorities such as the Hindu revivalists in India." Others emphasize the anti-imperialist nature of fundamentalism: they know it primarily as a reaction to Western forms of domination. Still others stress its anti-Communist emphasis to explain some aspects of North and South American Protestant fundamentalisms. Finally, some interpreters see fundamentalism as an expression of antimodernism, that is, as a reaction against the consequences of modernity, including the erosion of religious tradition, perverse applications of science and technology, and the deterioration of the spiritual and moral values once upheld by religious traditions.

The root cause of fundamentalist protest, according to a complementary school of thought, is the liberation of women from traditional gender roles. In fact, scholars such as the sociologist Martin Riesebrodt and the religion historian Helen Hardacre see fundamentalism primarily as a patriarchal protest movement attempting to restore traditional male roles to society. Fundamentalist discourses against abortion, coeducation, the unveiling of women, and, more generally, their full and equal participation in social, economic and political life are seen as reflecting this ill will against feminism.

Of course, there is no single explanation of fundamentalisms applicable to all cases; the specific issues on which fundamentalists have focused vary from society to society. Yet the antifeminist program of fundamentalists appears to be the most achievable of their many goals. To date, fundamentalists have enjoyed more success in influencing the intimate, personal aspects of life—controlling gender relations, the rearing of children and education—than in the larger, more diverse realm of courts, legislatures and battlefields (though they have had impressive success in these public zones as well).

Some interpreters of fundamentalism, in noting the irony of the surpassingly modern sensibilities of the antimodern fundamentalists, echoed the warning of French existentialist Jean-Paul Sartre: There is *No Exit* from the ambiguities and limitations of the human condition, including its cultural determinisms, to which fundamentalists ultimately fall prey, becoming just one more variation on the modernist theme. Other analysts have granted fundamentalism more integrity and originality, however. The British social philosopher Ernest Gellner sees it as one of the three powerful intellectual options available in the late twentieth century, the others being a permissive relativism ("postmodernism") and an enduring Enlightenment rationalism (or "rationalist fundamentalism").

Fundamentalists: Shrewd Social Observers

U.S. foreign policy experts are learning that fundamentalists are shrewd observers of the societies in which they live and can be reliable guides in finding the "fault lines" of a society and in alerting informed listeners to the problems or challenges looming on the horizon. Fundamentalisms in the Middle East, South Asia, Africa and North America are early-warning systems, launching cultural counterattacks against trends that would undermine society's moral foundations (as when fundamentalists in each of these regions attacked pornography in defense of the family and of "women's rights").

To Americans troubled by the growth of a morally impoverished (and armed) youth subculture of a permanent underclass in the United States, the analysis of the New Morality by Christian fundamentalist Bob Jones III, current president of Bob Jones University, may not sound as hysterical today as it did to some in 1968. Then he warned of "the debilitating philosophy of permissiveness" that would make people "take sin for granted" and cause us eventually to look upon hedonism, pornography, excessive materialism and blind ambition not as the means of corruption but "as a way of life that we must accept."

Fundamentalists' antennae also have picked up signals of corruption and approaching doom in Israel, where the shrewd diatribes of Gush Emunim rabbis appeal to Jews who worry that Judaism is being or has been replaced by secular Zionism as the "glue" that cements ethnic and personal identity. In Sunni Egypt and Shiite Iran, fundamentalists were among the first to criticize the eclectic process of state-building that occurred after World War II, when Western models of development were transplanted and adopted uncritically rather than gradually adapted to people with different historical traditions, experiences and values. People who are concerned about the future course of developing societies might well study the cultural criticism found in the sermons and tracts of fundamentalist leaders.

Fundamentalists are not only observers and critics of society's choices; they are also activists who propose alternative choices grounded in their religious worldviews. Much of the renewed attention, favorable and unfavorable, given to religion in the United States in the 1970s and 1980s was in large part inspired by fundamentalists' attempts to move into the mainstream of public debate. Gush Emunim-style fundamentalism occurred as segments of the Israeli population were drawn to Judaism in the euphoria following the 1967 Six-Day War. There was a renewed sense of national, ethnic and religious pride following the stunning Israeli victory over Arab adversaries.

While American Christianity appeared to go into a temporary eclipse in the 1960s, and while Israeli rabbis struggled to preserve Judaism as a religious as well as an ethnic identification, Islam never really lost its status as the cultural force that bequeaths legitimacy on governments in the Middle East, North Africa, parts of South Asia, Indonesia and Malaysia. Thus Islamic symbols and rhetoric have been appropriated by both fundamentalists and their opponents in the ongoing debate over the pace and direction of modernization and cultural development.

Having helped to restore or maintain religion's place in society, do fundamentalists gain widespread acceptance of their programs? The intensity of their protest and the absolutism of their religious language seem to have contradictory effects. On the one hand, secularists and other nonfundamentalists in Egypt, Israel and the United States certainly do not accept the entire package of metaphysics, religion and sociocultural criticism presented by fundamentalists; nonfundamentalists also tend to reject the tactics and the condemnations of the more radical fundamentalists. On the other hand, fundamentalists have reminded otherwise apathetic people that great issues demand response. Ironically,

UPI/Bettmann

Pat Robertson works a crowd of supporters at Bob Jones University on the eve of the South Carolina Republican primary, March 5, 1988. Robertson failed to win a single primary.

antipluralist fundamentalists have contributed to the expression of pluralism: their protests have spawned counterprotests by moderate or liberal believers and nonbelievers alike, initiating a wide-ranging and searching debate in the societies they seek to transform.

In April and May 1992, for example, Buffalo, N.Y., was the scene of a mass countermovement organized in response to Operation Rescue, which discovered that it was not the only protest group inspired by an oppositional mentality. The evangelical and fundamentalist Christians, including Roman Catholic antiabortionists, were confronted by pro-choice

69

activists and by the state, which arrested 597 protesters during the two-week "Spring of Life" operation. (Only a handful were abortion-rights advocates.) "We have been extremely effective," said Katherine Spillar of the Feminist Majority Foundation, a group that orchestrated defense plans for the five clinics under siege by Operation Rescue. "They have not accomplished anything." In Israel, a similar dynamic emerged in response to Jewish fundamentalism. Organizations like the lobbying group Peace Now have grown in numbers and influence in proportion to the perceived strength of the settler movement.

Fundamentalist movements vary significantly within each religious tradition. So it is with the nature of fundamentalist activism: not all fundamentalists express their disdain for secular society by breaking the law or by engaging in civil disobedience, especially in the United States, where other avenues of influence are open to dissenters. The Reverend Donald E. Wildmon leads an organization, the American Family Association, that plays by the rules of the game. Using market values and the courts to his advantage, Wildmon has organized Christian boycotts of advertisers who support "morally objectionable" television programs. In some notable instances, fundamentalist critiques of American society have been acknowledged by opponents on the left. People for the American Way, an organization that often lines up against fundamentalists in public debate, supports fundamentalist opposition to public-school textbooks that overlook religious themes in American society and American and world history.

It is difficult to remain a radical or hard-line fundamentalist in a democratic society precisely because there is usually someone listening to you, agreeing at least in part with your protest and willing to compromise on some points in order to join forces for the sake of increased political influence. That is one reason why some erstwhile Christian fundamentalists now prefer the label "neo-evangelical"; it better describes the approach of activist Christians who must keep their fundamentals to themselves a bit more when they enter into political coalitions, for example, with feminists against pornography or with moderate Roman Catholics against abortions.

Indeed, the attempt to characterize fundamentalisms across cultures leads to generalizations that must be examined in each case for exceptions and for modifications. In the first chapter, for example, it was noted that fundamentalists view crisis situations as an opportunity to awaken their undecided or ambivalent countrymen or coreligionists to the mortal threat to community and identity posed by liberal religion and/or by secular governments. The discussions on Christianity, Judaism and Islam described particular cultural crises that served as catalysts for fundamentalist beginnings or growth. To give them their due, however, it must be added that fundamentalists do not simply react to crises; the many successful movements such as the Muslim Brotherhood in Egypt and the Jamaat-e-Islami of Pakistan, and institutions such as Bob Jones University in Greenville, S.C., and the Mercaz Harav Yeshiva of ultra-Orthodox Judaism in Israel, do not depend on crises to sustain them. Fundamentalists are well-organized in preparation for crises and they understand basic human needs and meet them well. Sociologist Robert Wuthnow commented perceptively in the April 22, 1992, *Christian Century*:

> The success of fundamentalism is due also to the groups' ability to amass vast resources. Were they simply reacting to crises, they could not have lasting influence. But they are careful stewards of resources. They build colleges and seminaries when times are good. They train grass-roots leaders. By distinguishing themselves from outsiders, they make sure their followers spend time together, thinking about the right ideas and inculcating faith among the young. Indeed, modernity is very much their friend in this respect because it encourages them to think rationally, to plan ahead, to study, to engage in gainful employment, to strategize politically, and to model their own organizations on the businesses or government agencies in which they work.

Stereotypes about religious fundamentalisms remain strong, and many otherwise enlightened people continue to think of all fundamentalists as odd, threatening, regressive or barbarian—to take some of the more lighthearted terms used to describe them. To argue that fundamentalisms are constructive in spirit is not to deny that their programs begin with attacks, some of them fierce and unyielding, against a religious or political system, a mode of belief and practice, a liberal approach to sacred texts, or an irreligious life-style. Fundamentalists are reactive; they begin in an "anti" mode—antimodernist, antisecularist, antifeminist or anti-Communist.

But fundamentalist leaders are not mere protesters; they are innovative world-builders who act as well as react, who see a world that fails to meet their standards and then marshal resources in order to create an alternative world for their followers to inhabit and renew. In creating and sustaining an alternative world—whether it be the world of the Christian academy, the world of the West Bank settlement, or the Muslim Brotherhood chapter—fundamentalists are interactive. They are engaged in community-building, electioneering, political rallies and education, and they live amid other people who do not share their tenacious commitment to the religious "fundamentals." They worry about the growing secularity of their host societies and wish to restore God or, in the case of Hindu, Sikh and Buddhist fundamentalisms, some comparable conception of the divine, to a central place in the everyday consciousness of all people.

In this sense, fundamentalists are missionaries who, like all good missionaries, speak in the language of the people to whom the message is being addressed. They are enormously creative in formulating and modifying their ideas according to the needs and aspirations of ordinary people; as devotees of sacred texts and traditions, they know how to sustain a rich, common language that animates personal experience and forges bonds with other believers. Indeed, in Wuthnow's words, "fundamentalists' discursive and communal richness is a form of 'cultural capital,' giving people status within their religious communities much in the same way that wealth or education might give them prestige in the secular world."

As missionaries and world-builders, however, fundamentalists are inevitably concerned with the values of the times, which the British social philosopher Anthony Giddens has described as "late modernity." By this Giddens means a time of increasingly rapid acceleration of the processes unleashed by the high-tech revolution of this century, processes that have led late-modern institutions to "differ from all preceding forms of social order in respect of their dynamism, the degree to which they undercut traditional habits and customs, and their global impact." The consequences of the mass-communications technologies of late modernity alone suggest something of the extent of the transformation of self-consciousness and self-understanding that occurs when viewers and listeners around the world are exposed instantaneously to events, alternate cultures and a seemingly endless variety of choices of life-style and belief.

Media communicate these options in bits and pieces, often seemingly self-contained, which now exist independently of their former historical (time-space) context. In late modernity, Giddens says, one finds an increased level of self-awareness and an appreciation by people, especially community leaders and modern professional elites, of the ways in which identities can be "constructed" by a selective appropriation of elements from complex and once-coherent social systems. Among the social systems that are now being retrieved are the rich, detailed and previously well-integrated religious systems known as "traditions." Late modernity is thus parasitic, feeding on many different historical bodies; and these processes of late modernity are consciously or unconsciously internalized by people living in the cultures of late modernity—including fundamentalists.

Selectivity Is Key

Fundamentalists are constructive in this most modern of ways: they, too, draw upon selective bits of religious tradition and modernity. Fundamentalists fuse passages of sacred texts with modern political ideologies; they adopt bureaucratic organizational structures and resource-management techniques from the secularists who oppress them; they harness the latest technological innovations to fulfill ancient religious requirements. Fundamentalists idealize sacred lands, "freezing" them in time and place and thus lifting them out of their complex and changing historical contexts to serve as emblems of communal identity and as the *raison d'être* of political movements.

In this, fundamentalists are not to be singled out. As Giddens and other theorists have noted, almost every modern social movement follows this process of selection and identity construction. But fundamentalists construct their identities while claiming the special privilege of absolute authority: the revealed word of God escapes the erosion incumbent upon these processes. Although they may use modern instruments and processes, the fundamentalists argue, they are immune to the consequences of modernity because they are protected by a source of truth that is by definition outside of, over and above, time and space and the vicissitudes of history. The fundamentalist imagination is contained, however, when limits are set by civil society to the process of retrieving a past and constructing a future. The United States is notable in the twentieth century for its relative absence of religious violence, especially violence intended to undermine the constitution and governing foundational principles of the republic. Among polyglot and deeply pluralistic modern nations, the United States has been relatively successful in providing different immigrant groups, hailing from hundreds of regions and particular historical backgrounds, with essentially one national story and identity. The national myth has its founding hero-legend, George Washington; its sacred binding scriptures—the Constitution, Bill of Rights and Declaration of Independence; its saints and martyrs (Abraham Lincoln, John F. Kennedy and Martin Luther King); its national holidays (Fourth of July,

Veterans' Day, Memorial Day) and its most brilliant feature, a certain American pioneering open-endedness that allows for new ethnic heroes to fit in the mix: a black civil-rights leader, for example, or an Irish Catholic President.

This is precisely because the American founding ideal is revolutionary: that all are equal simply by being human; that competing interests, even if based on ethnic, racial or religious identities, must compete within this political-philosophical framework. James Madison predicted that no one sect or cult or party would win out in America because all parties, sects and cults could organize, speak freely, worship openly and promote political candidates—as long as they recognized the civil law and the rights upon which this creative, ordered pluralism was based. In other words, the key to America's success has been its ability to endorse competition as lawful, indeed as the very fiber of political and economic life; and to provide assurances, through a federal system and a semiwelfare state, that within that competition the losers retain full civil and political rights to participate. They are not, in theory at least, to be vanquished, exiled, executed, sold into slavery, or otherwise deprived of full rights. Those who lose the competition will not kill one another, nor will they revolt, but they will be administered by a federal government that benevolently restrains the play of the free market and attempts, with some degree of success, to weaken monopolistic political and economic powers.

Talking It Over

A Note for Students and Discussion Groups

This issue of the HEADLINE SERIES, like its predecessors, is published for every serious reader, specialized or not, who takes an interest in the subject. Many of our readers will be in classrooms, seminars or community discussion groups. Particularly with them in mind, we present below some discussion questions—suggested as a starting point only—and references for further reading.

Discussion Questions

Some experts claim that movements that invoke religious symbols and religious idioms only for political purposes are not fundamentalist. How would you differentiate between "religion as faith" and "religion as ideology"? Is there a clear distinction?

If religion is expressed as a political ideology, what aspects of religious doctrine must be changed, deleted or muted?

How do some religious fundamentalists explain the resort to violence? How do they justify violence in religious scriptural terms? in traditional terms?

Discuss the differences between scripture and codified law as forms of religiopolitical expression. How is religious scripture both more and less important to many fundamentalists than codified law?

Could "antifundamentalism"—the practice of denying believers certain rights as a result of their religious affiliations—be as dangerous to civil society as fundamentalism itself?

What are some of the possible political antidotes to radical, antidemocratic fundamentalisms?

What do the Christian, Hindu, Islamic and Jewish fundamentalist movements have in common? How do they differ?

READING LIST

Averill, Lloyd J., *Religious Right, Religious Wrong: A Critique of the Fundamentalist Phenomenon.* New York, Pilgrim Press, 1989. A Christian historian's meditation on the ways in which Christian fundamentalism distorts the traditional and scriptural teachings of the faith.

Caplan, Lionel, ed., *Studies in Religious Fundamentalism.* Albany, N.Y., State University of New York Press, 1988. A collection of anthropological case studies of religious resurgence in India, North America, the Middle East and East Africa.

Esposito, John L., *The Islamic Threat: Myth or Reality?* New York, Oxford University Press, 1992. Leading expert explores diversity of the Islamic resurgence and seeks to refute Western notions of a hostile, monolithic Islam.

Isaacs, Harold R., "Power and Identity: Tribalism in World Politics." *Headline Series* No. 246. New York, Foreign Policy Association, October 1979. Political scientist says that "differences in physical characteristics, language, history and origins, religion, nationality have produced the goriest aspects of most of human history."

Lawrence, Bruce B., *Defenders of God: The Fundamentalist Revolt Against the Modern Age.* San Francisco, Calif., Harper and Row, 1989. The first analytic comparative examination of fundamentalism in Christianity, Judaism and Islam.

Marty, Martin E., and Appleby, R. Scott, eds., four volumes of The Fundamentalism Project series already published by the University of Chicago Press: *Fundamentalisms Observed* (1991); *Fundamentalisms and Society: Reclaiming the Sciences, the Family, and Education* (1992); *Fundamentalisms and the State: Remaking Polities, Economies, and Militance* (1993); *Accounting for Fundamentalisms: The Dynamic Character of Movements* (1994).

Potter, Lawrence G., "Islam and Politics: Egypt, Algeria and Tunisia." *Great Decisions 1994*. New York, Foreign Policy Association, 1994. Three North African governments are under siege by Islamic militants. Why is this happening? How will it end?

"Religion in World Politics: Why the Resurgence?" *Great Decisions 1986*. New York, Foreign Policy Association, 1986. The article concludes that "for the United States, understanding the historical role and context of religious expression is the key to making accurate assessments of religious movements and formulating appropriate responses."

Rudolph, Susanne Hoeber, and Rudolph, Lloyd I., "Modern Hate." *The New Republic*, March 22, 1993. Political scientists at the University of Chicago discuss how ancient animosities get invented and give a case study of India's current convulsions.

Sahliyeh, Emile, ed., *Religious Resurgence and Politics in the Contemporary World*. Albany, N.Y., State University of New York Press, 1990. A collection of essays applying current sociological concepts such as "resource-mobilization theory" to the analysis of fundamentalistlike movements in Iran, Israel and the occupied territories, and Latin America, among others.

Zartman, I. William, and Habeeb, William M., eds., *Polity and Society in Contemporary North Africa*. Boulder, Colo., Westview Press, 1993. Overview of the transformations in North Africa since independence and current religious, economic, demographic and political trends.

Glossary

- **Bharatiya Janata party (BJP):** Hindu nationalist party, founded in 1980, is the main opposition to India's ruling Congress (I) party.

- **Granth Sahib:** Holy book considered by Sikhs to be the sole repository of spiritual authority; it has become an object of worship.

- **Gush Emunim ("Bloc of the Faithful"):** A group of nationalist and religiously observant Israeli settlers on the West Bank.

- **Hamas:** Popular name for the Islamic Resistance Movement, since 1989 a voice for the Islamic fundamentalist movement in the occupied territories, promoting confrontation with the Israeli authorities.

- **Islamic Salvation Front (FIS):** Organized in early 1989, it represented surging Islamic fundamentalist movement in Algeria.

- **National Liberation Front (FLN):** Founded in 1954, it was Algeria's only authorized political grouping in a one-party state until 1989, when constitutional changes led to the formation of nearly 60 legal parties.

- **Palestine Liberation Organization (PLO):** Created by Arab League in 1964 as an umbrella organization for various Palestinian groups, the PLO has been the leading spokesman for the Palestinian cause. Its longtime leader is Yasir Arafat.

- **Quran (Koran):** The sacred book of Islam, it was revealed to the Prophet Muhammad in separate revelations at Mecca and Medina during the Prophet's life.

- **Sharia:** Arabic for "way" or "path." Islamic law that theoretically governs all aspects of a Muslim's life. Quran (see above) is one of its main sources.

- **Shiite/Sunni Muslims:** Sunnis make up 90 percent of the world's Muslims; Shiites, about 10 percent. Sunnis, who predominate in the Arab world, believe Muslim leadership should be elective. Shiites, who predominate in Iran and Iraq, believe the Islamic leadership should remain within the family of the Prophet Muhammad through the descendants of his son-in-law, Ali.

- **Sikh:** Adherent of a monotheistic religion of India, marked by rejection of idolatry and caste; centered in the Indian state of Punjab.

- **Sufi:** A term pertaining to Muslim mystics, and their beliefs, practices and organizations.

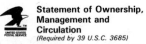

Statement of Ownership, Management and Circulation

(Required by 39 U.S.C. 3685)

1A. Title of Publication	1B. PUBLICATION NO.								2. Date of Filing
HEADLINE SERIES	0	0	1	7	8	7	8	0	3/25/94

3. Frequency of Issue	3A. No. of Issues Published Annually	3B. Annual Subscription Price
QUARTERLY: WINTER, SPRING, SUMMER, FALL	FOUR	$20.00

4. Complete Mailing Address of Known Office of Publication *(Street, City, County, State and ZIP+4 Code) (Not printers)*

FOREIGN POLICY ASSOCIATION, 729 Seventh Ave., NY NY 10019

5. Complete Mailing Address of the Headquarters of General Business Offices of the Publisher *(Not printer)*

SAME AS ABOVE

6. Full Names and Complete Mailing Address of Publisher, Editor, and Managing Editor *(This item MUST NOT be blank)*
Publisher *(Name and Complete Mailing Address)*

FOREIGN POLICY ASSOCIATION, 729 Seventh Ave., NY, NY 10019

Editor *(Name and Complete Mailing Address)*

NANCY HOEPLI, same as above

Managing Editor *(Name and Complete Mailing Address)*

N/A

7. Owner *(If owned by a corporation, its name and address must be stated and also immediately thereunder the names and addresses of stockholders owning or holding 1 percent or more of total amount of stock. If not owned by a corporation, the names and addresses of the individual owners must be given. If owned by a partnership or other unincorporated firm, its name and address, as well as that of each individual must be given. If the publication is published by a nonprofit organization, its name and address must be stated.) (Item must be completed.)*

Full Name	Complete Mailing Address
FOREIGN POLICY ASSOCIATION	729 Seventh Ave. NY NY 10019

8. Known Bondholders, Mortgagees, and Other Security Holders Owning or Holding 1 Percent or More of Total Amount of Bonds, Mortgages or Other Securities *(If there are none, so state)*

Full Name	Complete Mailing Address
N/A	N/A

9. For Completion by Nonprofit Organizations Authorized To Mail at Special Rates *(DMM Section 424.12 only)*
The purpose, function, and nonprofit status of this organization and the exempt status for Federal income tax purposes *(Check one)*

(1) ☒ Has Not Changed During Preceding 12 Months   (2) ☐ Has Changed During Preceding 12 Months   *(If changed, publisher must submit explanation of change with this statement.)*

10.	Extent and Nature of Circulation *(See instructions on reverse side)*	Average No. Copies Each Issue During Preceding 12 Months	Actual No. Copies of Single Issue Published Nearest to Filing Date
A.	Total No. Copies *(Net Press Run)*	8147	7991
B.	Paid and/or Requested Circulation 1. Sales through dealers and carriers, street vendors and counter sales	765	259
	2. Mail Subscription *(Paid and/or requested)*	2526	2299
C.	Total Paid and/or Requested Circulation *(Sum of 10B1 and 10B2)*	3291	2558
D.	Free Distribution by Mail, Carrier or Other Means Samples, Complimentary, and Other Free Copies	572	364
E.	Total Distribution *(Sum of C and D)*	3863	2922
F.	Copies Not Distributed 1. Office use, left over, unaccounted, spoiled after printing	4284	5069
	2. Return from News Agents	- 0 -	- 0 -
G.	TOTAL *(Sum of E, F1 and 2—should equal net press run shown in A)*	8147	7991

11.
I certify that the statements made by me above are correct and complete

Signature and Title of Editor, Publisher, Business Manager, or Owner

Lisa Siuri-Ardemucci

Executive Director of Finance and Administration

PS Form **3526**, January 1991   *(See instructions on reverse)*